T0215039

Practical WebDriverIO

Learn to Automate Effectively Using WebDriverIO APIs

Shashank Shukla

Apress®

Practical WebDriverIO

Shashank Shukla
Mandla, India

ISBN-13 (pbk): 978-1-4842-6660-1   ISBN-13 (electronic): 978-1-4842-6661-8
https://doi.org/10.1007/978-1-4842-6661-8

Managing Director, Apress Media LLC: Welmoed Spahr
Acquisitions Editor: Louise Corrigan
Development Editor: James Markham
Coordinating Editor: Nancy Chen

Cover designed by eStudioCalamar

Cover image by Jimmy Chan from Pexels

Distributed to the book trade worldwide by Springer Science+Business Media New York, 1 New York Plaza, New York, NY 10004. Phone 1-800-SPRINGER, fax (201) 348-4505, e-mail orders-ny@springer-sbm.com, or visit www.springeronline.com. Apress Media, LLC is a California LLC and the sole member (owner) is Springer Science + Business Media Finance Inc (SSBM Finance Inc). SSBM Finance Inc is a **Delaware** corporation.

For information on translations, please e-mail booktranslations@springernature.com; for reprint, paperback, or audio rights, please e-mail bookpermissions@springernature.com

Apress titles may be purchased in bulk for academic, corporate, or promotional use. eBook versions and licenses are also available for most titles. For more information, reference our Print and eBook Bulk Sales web page at http://www.apress.com/bulk-sales.

Any source code or other supplementary material referenced by the author in this book is available to readers on GitHub via the book's product page, located at www.apress.com/9781484266601. For more detailed information, please visit http://www.apress.com/source-code.

Printed on acid-free paper

*This book is dedicated to my mom and dad
for always loving and supporting me.*

Table of Contents

About the Author .... **xxv**

About the Technical Reviewer .... **xxvii**

Acknowledgments .... **xxix**

Introduction .... **xxxi**

Chapter 1: Getting Started **1**

Introduction 1

Installation 2

    Prerequisites 3

    Installation process 4

    Additional Information 13

Summary 14

Chapter 2: Web Locators **15**

ID 20

    Syntax 21

    Output 21

Class 21

    Syntax 21

    Output 22

    Notes 22

Name Attribute 25

    Syntax...26

    Output...26

    Notes 26

Tag Name 26

    Syntax...27

    Output...27

Link Text..28

    Syntax...28

    Output...28

    Note 28

Partial Link Text...29

    Syntax...29

    Output...29

    Note 29

Elements with Certain Text 30

    Syntax...30

CSS Query Selector...31

    Syntax...31

    Output...32

    Note 32

XPath...32

    Syntax...33

    Output...33

    Note 33

JS Function 34

    Syntax...34

    Output...35

Chain Selectors 35

 Syntax 35

 Output 35

 Note 36

React Selectors 36

 Syntax 37

 Notes 37

Custom Selectors 38

 Syntax 38

 Output 39

 Notes 39

Summary 39

Chapter 3: Browser APIs 41

Debugging 42

 Syntax 43

 Output 43

 Notes 44

Loading URL and Basic Authentication 44

 Output 45

 Notes 46

Getting a Count of the Elements Returned from an Array of Elements 46

 Syntax 46

 Output 47

 Notes 47

Getting the First Element Returned from an Array of Elements 47

 Syntax 48

 Output 48

 Notes 48

Getting the Text of an Element 49

    Syntax 49

    Output 50

    Notes 50

Getting the Text of any Element Returned from an Array of Elements 50

    Syntax 50

    Output 51

    Notes 51

Getting the Last Element Returned from an Array of Elements 51

    Syntax 51

    Output 52

Iterating All Elements 52

    Syntax 52

    Output 53

    Notes 54

Getting All the Links on a Page 54

    Syntax 54

    Code Snippet 54

    Output 55

    Notes 55

Map Function 55

    Syntax 55

    Output 56

    Notes 56

Scrolling an Element into View 58

    Syntax 58

    Output 58

    Notes 59

Click an Element 59

    Syntax...60

    Output...60

    Notes 60

Double-Click an Element..61

    Syntax...62

    Output...62

    Notes 63

Right-Clicking an Element 63

    Syntax...63

    Output...63

    Notes 64

Sending Text to an Input Field...64

    Syntax...64

    Output...64

    Notes 65

Sending a Text to an Input Field via addValue...65

    Syntax...65

    Output...66

Sending Keyboard Keys to an Element 66

    Syntax...66

    Output...67

    Notes 67

Getting the Value of an Element...67

    Syntax...67

    Output...68

    Notes 68

Clearing the Text Inside an Input Field 68

    Syntax 68

    Output 69

Hovering the Mouse on an Element 69

    Syntax 69

    Output 70

    Notes 70

Navigating to a New URL in a Browser 71

    Syntax 71

    Output 71

    Notes 71

Navigating Back in a Browser 72

    Syntax 72

    Output 72

    Notes 73

Navigating Forward in a Browser 73

    Syntax 73

    Output 74

Refreshing a Web Page 74

    Syntax 74

    Output 75

    Notes 75

Restarting a Browser 75

    Syntax 76

    Output 76

Getting and Setting Window Size and Position 76

    Syntax...77

    Output...79

    Notes 79

Getting Element Size...79

    Syntax...79

    Output...80

    Notes 80

Maximizing the Browser 80

    Syntax...81

    Output...82

    Notes 83

Minimizing the Browser..83

    Syntax...83

    Output...84

    Notes 84

Browser Fullscreen Mode 84

    Syntax...84

    Output...85

Opening a New Window 85

    Syntax...85

    Output...86

    Notes 86

Getting the URL of the Current Page 86

    Syntax...86

    Output...87

Sending JavaScript to do a Task: Vanilla JS Code...87

    Syntax..87

    Output..88

    Notes...88

Sending JavaScript to do a Task: Handling Datepicker.....................................88

    Syntax..89

    Output..89

    Notes...89

Taking a Full-Page Screenshot 90

    Syntax..90

    Output..90

    Notes...90

Switching Between Windows...90

    Syntax..91

    Output..91

    Notes...91

Switching Between Frames 92

    Syntax..92

    Output..93

    Notes...94

Closing the Page 94

    Syntax..94

    Output..95

    Notes...95

Closing the Browser 96

    Syntax..96

    Output..96

    Notes...96

Alerts: Accepting an Alert 97

    Syntax 97

    Output 98

    Notes 98

Alerts: Dismissing an Alert 98

    Syntax 98

    Output 99

    Notes 99

Alerts: Sending a Message to an Alert 100

    Syntax 100

    Output 101

    Notes 101

Alerts: Reading an Alert Message 101

    Syntax 102

    Output 102

    Notes 102

Selecting from a Drop-Down 102

    Syntax 103

    Output 104

Drag and Drop 105

    Syntax 105

    Output 105

    Notes 106

Uploading a File 107

    Output 108

    Notes 108

Submitting a Form 108

    Notes 108

Display Cookies 108

   Syntax 109

   Output 109

   Notes 110

Delete Cookies 110

   Syntax 110

   Output 110

   Notes 111

Set Cookies 111

   Syntax 111

   Output 112

   Notes 112

Geolocations 113

   Syntax 114

   Output 115

   Notes 115

Summary 116

Chapter 4: Element APIs and WebdriverIO Assertions 117

Is the Element Present?: isExisting() 118

   Syntax 118

   Output 119

   Notes 120

Is the Element Present?: toExist() 120

   Syntax 120

   Output 121

   Notes 121

Is the Element Present?: toBePresent()...122

    Syntax...122

    Output...122

    Note...123

Is the Element Present in DOM?: ToBeExisting()...........................123

    Syntax...123

    Output...124

    Notes...124

Is the Element Enabled?: IsEnabled()..124

    Syntax...125

    Output...126

    Notes...126

Is the Element Enabled?: toBeEnabled()..126

    Syntax...127

    Output...127

    Notes...127

Is the Element Disabled?: toBeDisabled()..128

    Syntax...128

    Output...129

    Notes...129

Is the Element Visible?: isDisplayed()..129

    Syntax...130

    Output...130

    Notes...131

Is the Element Visible?: toBeDisplayed()..132

    Syntax...132

    Output...132

    Notes...133

Is the Element Visible?: toBeVisible()..133

    Syntax...133

    Output...133

Is the Element Visible on the screen?: toBeDisplayedInViewport()...................134

    Syntax...134

    Output...134

    Notes 135

Is the Element Visible on the Screen?: toBeVisibleInViewport() 135

    Syntax...135

    Output...136

Is the Element Selected?: isSelected() 136

    Syntax...137

    Output...138

    Notes 138

Is the Element Selected?: toBeSelected()...138

    Syntax...138

    Output...139

Is the Element Selected?: toBeChecked()...139

    Syntax...139

    Output...140

Is the Element Clickable?: isClickable()..141

Syntax 141

    Output...142

    Notes 142

Is the Element Clickable?: toBeClickable() 142

    Syntax...142

    Output...143

    Notes 143

To Sum It Up...143

Summary...146

Chapter 5: Additional WebdriverIO Methods 147

Is the Element Focused?: isFocused...148

Syntax...148

Output...149

Note 149

Is the Element Focused?: toBeFocused 149

Syntax...150

Output...150

Note 150

Does the Element Have a Specific Attribute?: toHaveAttribute......................151

Syntax...151

Output...152

Notes 152

Does the Element Have a Specific Attribute?: toHaveAttr.............................152

Syntax...153

Output...153

Does the Element Contain a Specific Text Attribute?:
toHaveAttributeContaining 154

Syntax...154

Output...155

Notes 155

Does the Element Have a Specific Class?: toHaveClass 155

Syntax...156

Output...156

Notes 157

Does the Element Contain Specific Text in Class?: toHaveClassContaining......157

    Syntax...157

    Output...158

    Notes..159

Does the Element Have a Specific Property?: toHaveElementProperty 159

    Syntax...160

    Output...160

    Notes..160

Does the Element Have a Specific Value?: toHaveValue 161

    Syntax...161

    Output...161

    Notes..162

Does the Element Have a Specific href?: toHaveHref 162

    Syntax...162

    Output...162

    Notes..163

Does the Element Contain a Specific Text in the href?:
toHaveHrefContaining 163

    Syntax...163

    Output...164

Does the Element Have a Specific Link?: toHaveLink....................................164

    Syntax...164

    Output...165

    Notes..165

Does the Element Contain a Specific Text in the Link?:
toHaveLinkContaining 165

    Syntax...165

    Output...166

    Notes..166

Does the Element Have a Specific Text?: toHaveText..............................166

    Syntax..166

    Output..167

    Notes 167

Does the Element Contain a Specific Text?: toHaveTextContaining()..............167

    Syntax..168

    Output..168

Does the Element Have a Specific ID? 168

    Syntax..168

    Output..169

Element Count..169

    Syntax..170

    Output..170

    Notes 170

To Sum It Up...171

Summary..174

Chapter 6: Other Useful APIs 175

Dealing with a Shadow DOM..175

    Syntax..177

    Output..178

Getting the Page Source 181

    Syntax..181

    Output..181

Getting an Active Element 181

    Syntax..182

    Output..182

Getting the Property of an Element..182

    Syntax..182

    Output..183

Getting the CSS Property of an Element 184

    Syntax..184

    Output..185

Getting the Tag Name of an Element..186

    Syntax..186

    Output..186

Getting the Location of an Element..186

    Syntax..187

    Output..187

Getting the Size of an Element..188

    Syntax..188

    Output..189

Getting the HTML Build of an Element 189

    Syntax..189

    Output..190

Summary..190

Chapter 7: Waits 191

Hard and Explicit Waits at a Glance 191

Hard Sleep 192

    Syntax..192

    Output..192

Wait for an Element to Be Clickable..193

    Syntax..193

    Output..194

Wait for an Element to Be Displayed...194

    Syntax...195

    Output...196

Wait for an Element to Be Enabled 197

    Syntax...197

    Output...198

Wait for an Element to Exist..198

    Syntax...199

    Output...200

Wait Until...200

    Syntax...200

    Output...201

    Summary...202

Chapter 8: Timeouts 203

Setting and Getting Various Timeouts...204

    Output...204

Session Implicit Wait Timeout...205

Session Page Load Timeout...206

Output 207

Session Script Timeout 207

WebdriverIO-related Timeouts: waitforTimeout 208

Output 209

Framework-related Timeouts...209

Summary..211

Chapter 9: Framework Options and Design Patterns.........................213

Introduction to Frameworks...213

WebdriverIO with Cucumber 214

WebdriverIO with TypeScript...217

WebdriverIO with Jasmine 218

    WebdriverIO with Mocha 218

Design Pattern Introduction 219

    base.js 221

    login.page.js 222

    landing.page.js 224

    example.e2e.js 225

Summary...226

Chapter 10: Assertions 229

Determining If Strings Match by Value...230

Determining If Strings Match by Value and Type....................................230

Determining If a Value Is Truthy 231

Determining If a Value Is Falsy...231

Determining If a Value Is Equal (==) 231

Determining If a Value and Type Both Are Equal (===)...........................232

Determining If a Value Is Not Equal (==)...233

Determining If a Value and Type Are Not Equal (==)...............................233

Determining If a Value Is Higher Than Expected 234

Determining If a Value Is Lower 234

Determining If Expected Is True 235

Determining If Expected Is False 235

Determining If Expected Result Is an Array..235

Determining If an Actual Result Is a String 236

Determining If an Array Contains a Value..236

Verifying the Length of an Array...237

Summary...237

Chapter 11: Configuration File...239

Runner 240

Specs 241

Exclude 241

logLevel..242

Services 242

Reporters 244

Capabilities 248

Summary...253

Chapter 12: Conclusion...255

Advantages of WebdriverIO 256

Disadvantages of WebdriverIO 259

Challenges of Using WebdriverIO 260

Index..263

About the Author

Shashank Shukla has been working in software testing for more than a decade and is passionate about tools and technologies that can be leveraged to enrich the testing experience and optimize the quality of delivery. This is his first book.

About the Technical Reviewer

Kanika Sud has been working on the Web for more than ten years. Her work spans enterprise CMSes in Java, back-end technologies in the LAMP stack, and the MEAN stack. She has also worked on open source e-commerce CMSes and UX strategy. Solution design remains her favorite job. Market research on mobile apps and plugins led her to experiment with a bootstrapped technology startup called Codnostic Solutions. Find her on LinkedIn at `www.linkedin.com/in/kanikasud`.

Acknowledgments

I would like to thank all the generous people in the open source community for tirelessly contributing to making WebdriverIO easy to use, and helping others implement smarter testing approaches.

I want to thank my wife, Anuja, who encouraged me to write this book and supported me throughout the writing process, and my son, Riyaarth, for teaching me not to let "the lack of time" hold me back.

I would also like to thank my test manager, Eileen Stevenson, for her leadership and guidance, and also my test team, Anju, Gomathi, Shilpa, Mueez, Sreekanth, Kay and Lucie for always being there to support me.

And lastly, I want to thank my editorial team for their interest and effort, which fine-tuned and shaped this book.

Introduction

WebdriverIO is probably the coolest NodeJS-based framework gathering traction in the market. It has simplified complex, promise-based testing that stems due to the asynchronous nature of JavaScript in NodeJS-based frameworks. This tool saves time in automating websites and is fun to use. This book attempts to condense WebdriverIO's API documentation with practical, easy-to-understand examples. This book is a one-stop reference guide on almost every desktop API provided by WebdriverIO.

The journey starts with setting up the WebdriverIO test tool. You learn how to install it and its related dependencies and run a demo spec file in Chapter 1. In Chapter 2, you learn the methods to locate elements using various selector strategies provided by WebdriverIO, which are essential in interacting with web elements.

Chapters 3, 4, 5, and 6 explore various WebdriverIO API methods through easy-to-understand examples of automating a variety of user actions on located elements and the web app. You also learn some of WebdriverIO's built-in assertions.

In Chapter 7, you learn the importance of the wait command in automation testing and implement various wait commands. In Chapter 8, you learn about timeouts. After covering enough groundwork, the book touches upon various WebdriverIO framework options.

You learn about the page object model design pattern in Chapter 9. In Chapter 10, you learn about an external assertion library called the Chai Assertion Library. You then learn about WebdriverIO configuration settings and how to integrate a reporter and parallelly execute tests in Chapter 11.

The journey concludes in Chapter 12 by looking at some of the pros and cons of WebdriverIO.

CHAPTER 1

Getting Started

If you're interested in browser automation through Node.js and understanding the various methods that can be employed to effectively automate user actions on your web site, this book is for you. WebdriverIO is a fast-growing automation tool that is hard to ignore as Node.js/ JavaScript technologies assert their dominance in front-end and back-end web development.

This chapter briefly introduces WebdriverIO. You learn how to install it and quickly get to a point where you can start hands-on work. The chapter also discusses the following.

- Why WebdriverIO is gaining popularity among a new generation of test engineers

- How to run a test in 15 minutes

- Steps to take if the installation fails

- Demo web sites to practice test automation

Introduction

WebdriverIO is an independent and customized implementation of WebDriverJS (Selenium WebDriver) created by Christian Bromann. WebDriverJS is the official JavaScript implementation of Selenium API, packaged as 'selenium-webdriver' in npm, which runs on Node.js. WebdriverIO abstracts the lengthy syntax and complex asynchronous

© Shashank Shukla 2021
S. Shukla, *Practical WebDriverIO*, https://doi.org/10.1007/978-1-4842-6661-8_1

promise management of JavaScript and presents the user with easy-to-read action commands. It makes every test step synchronous, meaning the user doesn't have to worry about any missed steps in the test code. It is very flexible, allowing users to choose assertion libraries, reporting tools, and various other components of the framework.

WebdriverIO is packaged and installed through npm and runs on Node.js, which is a JavaScript run-time environment that allows you to run JavaScript outside your browser. It can run on macOS, Linux, and Windows.

The principal reason WebdriverIO is gaining traction is that it is open source. If you have experience working with other JavaScript frameworks, you can start using this tool in no time. Figure 1-1 shows its number of downloads over the past few years, depicting its growing popularity.

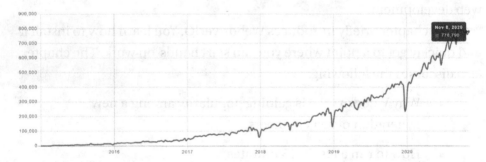

Figure 1-1. *The growing popularity of WebdriverIO (from* www.*npmtrends.com)*

Installation

The WebdriverIO installation process is very easy. This book explains installation in the Windows 10 operating system. You need an active Internet connection and enough space on your machine to accommodate the setup.

Prerequisites

This section describes the basic tools required for a barebones WebdriverIO project setup.

Node.js

The official Node.js download page is at `https://nodejs.org/en/download/`. You can download the LTS (latest stable version) or the current version with the latest Node.js features. It is strongly advised to download the LTS version so that you can avoid unforeseen errors due to experimental features in the package. If you are using Node.js for the first time, it is advisable to download to the location suggested by your operating system. This applies to all the tools I recommend you install in this book. I have used Node.js version 12.16.3 (`https://nodejs.org/en/blog/release/v12.16.3/`) in this book. I recommend you use the same to avoid any errors due to version mismatch.

VS Code

In the JavaScript universe, VS Code is a widely used, freely available code editor. It provides good integration and support with WebdriverIO for our test development. It is frequently updated with new features to make a developer's life easy. I use version 1.49 in this book. You are free to use the latest available version because it does not impact your execution (`https://code.visualstudio.com/download`).

Chrome

WebdriverIO provides flexibility to use a wide variety of browsers. Chrome (`www.google.com/chrome`) is used in this book because it is most convenient. Specifically, this book uses Chrome version 87.

Note that if you are using the latest version of Node.js, you might be asked to install Python or JDK as part of the installation process. I recommend installing the versions used in this book.

3

Installation process

Once you get these applications installed, create a folder named WebdriverIO_0709 or any name of your choosing, and open that folder via VS Code by right-clicking it, as depicted in Figure 1-2.

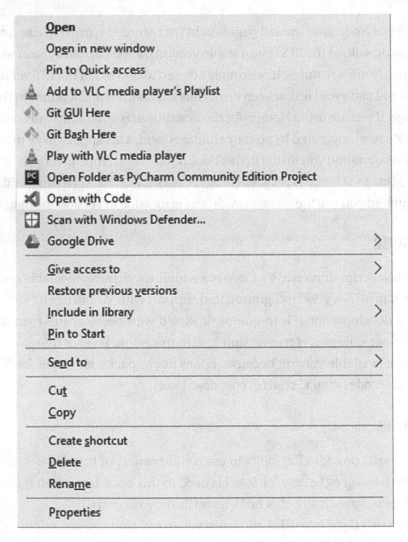

Open
Open in new window
Pin to Quick access
🔺 Add to VLC media player's Playlist
🔷 Git GUI Here
🔷 Git Bash Here
🔺 Play with VLC media player
🅿️ Open Folder as PyCharm Community Edition Project
❌ Open with Code
⊞ Scan with Windows Defender...
🔺 Google Drive   >

Give access to   >
Restore previous versions
Include in library   >
Pin to Start

Send to   >

Cut
Copy

Create shortcut
Delete
Rename

Properties

Figure 1-2. *VS Code options when right-clicked*

You can check the Node.js installation and version by opening your command prompt and typing **node -v**, as shown in Figure 1-3. This confirms that Node.js is installed in your system.

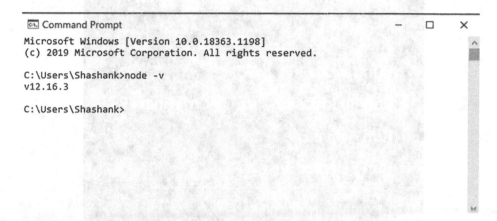

Figure 1-3. *Checking Node.js version in command prompt*

Once the VS Code is launched, click the Terminal option in the VS Code menu bar, and click New Terminal, as shown in Figure 1-4. The *terminal* is the command prompt embedded in the VS Code.

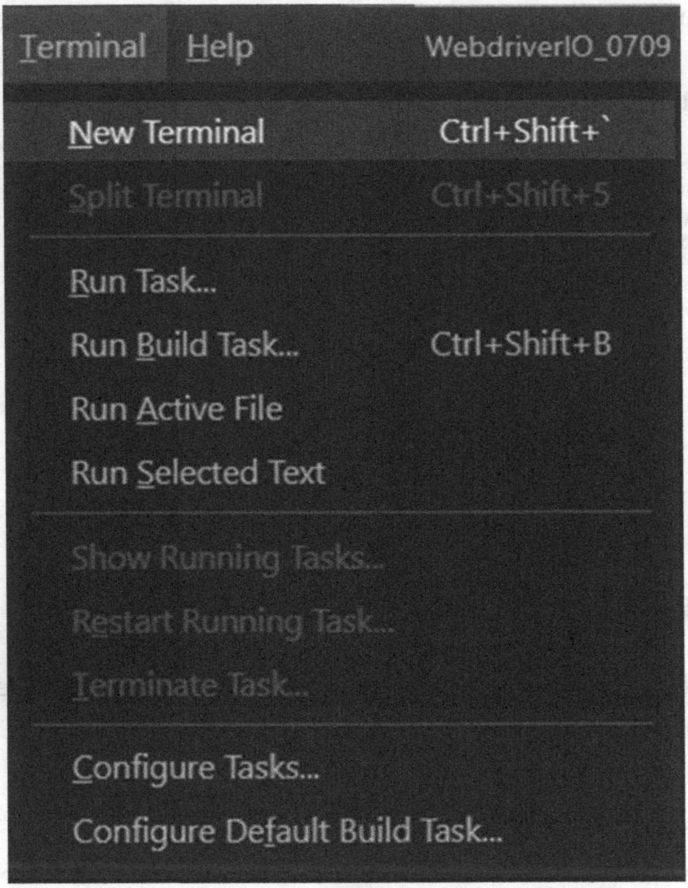

Figure 1-4. *VS Click the New Terminal option*

In the newly opened terminal, type the following command to initiate a node project. It creates a package.json file that manages all your project dependencies, as shown in Figure 1-5.

```
npm init -y
```

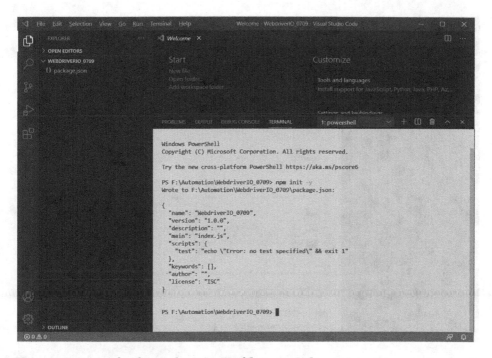

Figure 1-5. *Default package.json file created*

Use the following command to install WebdriverIO and its test runner, which enables you to start testing.

```
npm install @wdio/cli@6.8.0 --save-dev
```

To understand what this command does, you need to know what npm is. The *node package manager* can be compared to Google Play Store. Similar to downloading apps from Play Store, you can get any package developed and published by any Node.js programmer included in your Node.js application. The command calls `WDIO CLI via npm`, and using the @ symbol, it specifies the `6.8.0` version of the package. It needs to be saved to a local repository as a dev dependency, as shown in Figure 1-6. If you want to access it across any project on your Windows machine, provide the –g parameter and install it globally. WDIO CLI comprises other components, which we will see shortly.

7

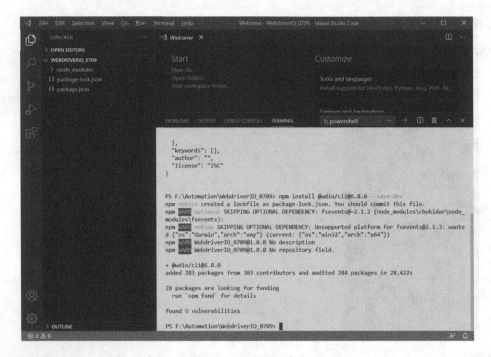

Figure 1-6. *wdio/cli installation successful*

Next, run the WebdriverIO configuration command with all the default inputs (-y parameter). I removed additional logs to keep things clean (see Figure 1-7). If you see additional logs at your end, don't panic.

```
npx wdio config -y
```

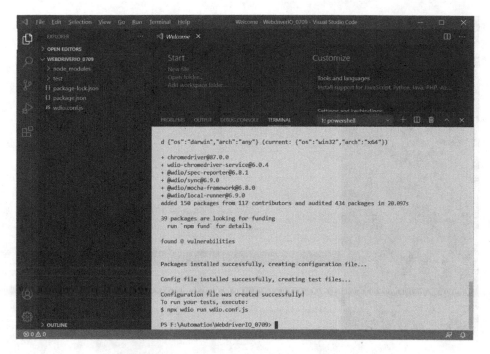

Figure 1-7. *WebdriverIO successful configuration*

WebdriverIO automatically creates a file structure for you.

The pageobjects folder is also created, as shown in Figure 1-8, demonstrating that WebdriverIO's creators strongly endorse the Page Object Model design pattern to manage test scripts in this framework. The purpose of the Page Object Model is to completely encapsulate the web page's testing interface in one place, which is a .js file in this case. The tester should understand that if a change is made on a specific web page in the web site, the automation suite requires corresponding changes.

The Page Object Model also abstracts all irrelevant information from the actual tests so that your test cases are legible. Unnecessary details like locators, test data, or functions can be hidden from the tester.

The Page Object Model is briefly mentioned later in this book because the primary focus of this book is to familiarize you with the API methods available in WebdriverIO to automate user interaction with web pages. If you want, you can delete the pageobjects folder for simplicity's sake.

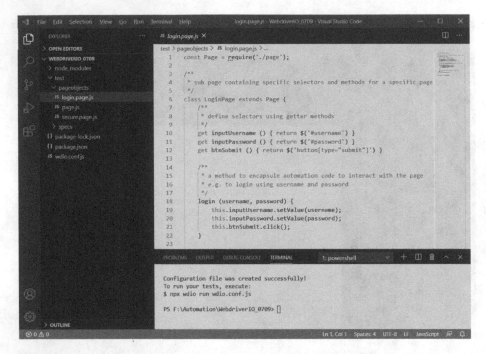

Figure 1-8. *Page object abstracts locators and functions from the main test*

Go to test ➤ specs ➤ example.e2e.js, as shown in Figure 1-9. This is where this book operates most of the time. It's called a *spec file*.

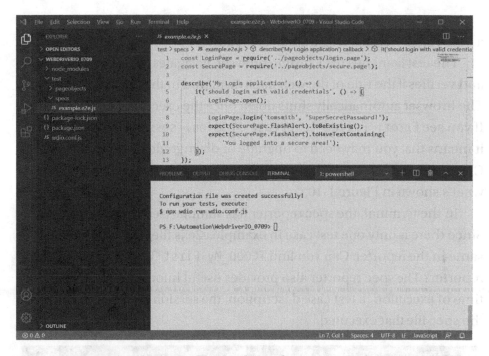

Figure 1-9. *example.e2e.js file is where the test cases be written*

Delete the contents of the file, copy the code provided in Listing 1-1, paste it in your example.e2e.js file, and save it.

Listing 1-1. A Sample Code Snippet Opens Google.com and Asserts the Web Site Title to Google String

```
describe('Webdriver.io examples', () => {
    it('TC000_My First Test Case', () => {
        browser.url('https://www.google.com/')
        expect(browser).toHaveTitle('Google')
    })
})
```

Run your first script using the following command.

```
npx wdio wdio.conf.js
```

If you see the browser spinning up in your machine, congrats, you have a barebones WebdriverIO framework ready.

The test launches the Chrome browser, navigates to Google.com, and verifies if the title of the web page displayed in the title bar is *Google*. The browser automatically shuts down once the execution is complete. If you see `Error: Failed to create session. session not created:`, it means that you may need to upgrade or downgrade your version of Chrome to version 87. At this point, your project/framework should look what's shown in Figure 1-10.

In the terminal, the spec reporter has summarized the test execution. Since there is only one test case in example.e2e.js file, you can find the same in the reporter. Can you find `TC000_My First Test Case` in the spec reporter? The spec reporter also provides useful information such as the time of execution, a test case description, the session ID, and the name of the spec file that executed.

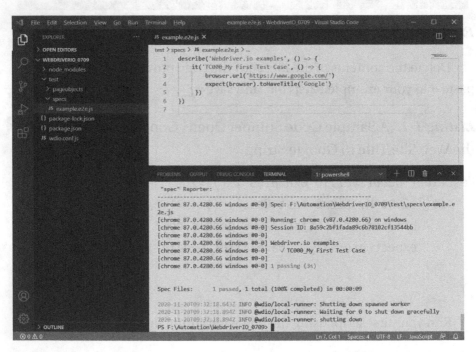

Figure 1-10. *Successful run of the first test*

Additional Information

Versioning mismatch can be a real pain in Node.js/JavaScript-based frameworks. If you are unable to run the test script after following the preceding steps, copy the devDependencies provided in Listing 1-2 and paste it into your package.json file, replacing the one that you have. Fire up the npm update command in the terminal to ensure that you are using all the dependency versions shown in the book, or upgrade everything to their latest versions.

Listing 1-2. List of Dependencies in This Project

```
"devDependencies": {
  "@wdio/cli": "^6.8.0",
  "@wdio/local-runner": "^6.9.0",
  "@wdio/mocha-framework": "^6.8.0",
  "@wdio/spec-reporter": "^6.8.1",
  "@wdio/sync": "^6.9.0",
  "chromedriver": "^87.0.0",
  "wdio-chromedriver-service": "^6.0.4"
}
```

wdio/cli is WebdriverIO's test runner. wdio/local-runner runs the tests in the local machine. Mocha-framework organizes the test cases with the help of 'describe' and 'it' block syntax. spec-reporter is a WebdriverIO plugin to report the spec in your terminal after the test executes. wdio/sync is a helper module to synchronously run WebdriverIO commands.

ChromeDriver is a standalone server that implements W3C web driver standards, and Selenium WebDriver uses it to control Chrome. As per WebdriverIO's official web site, this service seamlessly runs ChromeDriver when you run tests with the WDIO test runner.

Summary

This chapter introduced WebdriverIO, explained how to install it, and listed its installation prerequisites.

In the next chapter, you learn about locators are and how elements are uniquely identified in WebdriverIO.

We use the following demo web sites.

- `https://ultimateqa.com`

- `https://saucedemo.com`

- `https://the-internet.herokuapp.com`

- `https://jqueryui.com`

The first three web sites can be used to practice the examples provided in this book and automation in general. They are not likely to change anytime soon, so the examples remain intact and relevant no matter when you refer to them.

Without any further ado, let's start looking at elements with locators in WebdriverIO.

CHAPTER 2

Web Locators

Now that you have your framework installed, and the first test case is
successfully running, let's proceed to the next logical step. In this chapter,
you learn how to locate the elements of a web page to interact with them.
You also learn different locator strategies and how WebdriverIO uniquely
uses them. The chapter discusses the following.

- Taking a screenshot of an identified element

- ID locator

- Class locator

- Name locator

- Tag name locator

- Link text locator

- Partial link text locator

- Element with certain text locator

- CSS query selector locator

- XPath locator

- Using a vanilla JS function as a locator

- Chaining different locators

- React locators

- Making custom locators

© Shashank Shukla 2021
S. Shukla, *Practical WebDriverIO*, https://doi.org/10.1007/978-1-4842-6661-8_2

Web pages are written in HyperText Markup Language, or HTML. Cascading Style Sheets beautify web pages. JavaScript brings the pages to life by making them dynamic. Any web page is a mix of these three foundational technologies. A web page is comprised of multiple elements. To interact with a web page, you should know which operation to send to which element, and for that, it is necessary to uniquely identify an element.

Locators are the foundation of any automation. With the help of a locator strategy, you can uniquely identify an element you need to interact with among numerous other elements present on a web page. A robust test script has uniquely identifiable elements that remain unchanged throughout the product's development.

First, let's learn how to take a screenshot of an element. With the ability to take screenshots in your arsenal, you can accurately ensure if elements identified by your locator strategy are as expected.

The demo practice web site by Ultimate QA is shown in Figure 2-1.

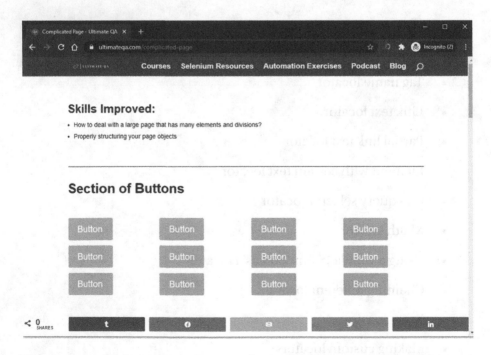

Figure 2-1. *Ultimate QA demo web site for automation practice*

Let's fetch this web site's logo (i.e., the first element in the nav bar) and capture a screenshot.

In Listing 2-1, the code finds the element and saves the screenshot via the saveScreenshot API.

Listing 2-1. First Line Inside the it Block Gets the URL, Second Line Pauses the execution for 3 seconds and Third line Locates the Element and Saves Its Screenshot

```
it('TC001_Taking Element Screenshot', () => {
    browser.url('https://ultimateqa.com/complicated-page/')
    browser.pause(3000)
    $('#logo').saveScreenshot('Screenshots/TC001.png')
})
```

Comment out the earlier it block in your example.e2e.js file and create a folder named Screenshots in your project's root directory. I deleted the pageobjects folder and renamed the example.e2e.js file as basic.js for simplicity. Your basic.js file and framework should look similar to Figure 2-2.

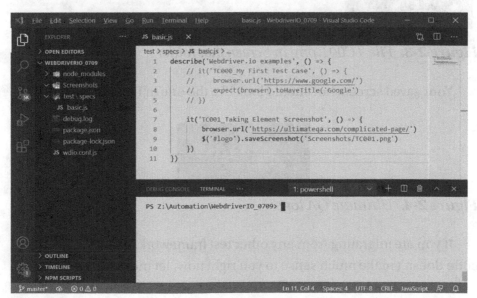

Figure 2-2. *Framework with screenshot capability addition*

When you run this via the following command, you should see your browser spinning up and closing down.

```
npx wdio wdio.conf.js
```

A screenshot is saved, as shown in Figure 2-3.

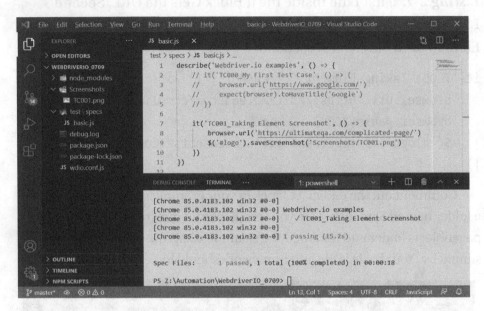

Figure 2-3. *File TC001.png in Screenshot folder*

Your saved screenshot should look like the one in Figure 2-4.

Figure 2-4. *Ultimate QA logo*

If you are migrating from any other test framework, and the preceding code doesn't make much sense to you right now, let me dissect it a little.

When you installed WebdriverIO, Mocha was part of the installation. If you want to verify it, refer to your package.json file, where you find the following entry.

```
"@wdio/mocha-framework": "^6.1.19",
```

This means you are using the Mocha Framework. Do not confuse WebdriverIO and Mocha. WebdriverIO is a browser automation framework. Mocha is a unit test framework for Node. It primarily *organizes* your test cases so that you don't have to go through random lines of code to determine where a test case starts and where it ends!

For more information on the differences between WebdriverIO and Mocha, refer to https://knapsackpro.com/testing_frameworks/difference_between/webdriver-io/vs/mochajs.

describe creates a suite of test cases with the help of it blocks; that is, it blocks are an implementation of a single test case. The first argument in an it block is an explanation/description of the test case. The next argument is the code, which is a JavaScript arrow function (()=>). An arrow function simplifies the syntax in Mocha as the functions in it, and describe blocks are anonymous functions. Multiple it blocks may be inside one describe block, as you saw in Figure 2-3. You can have nested describe blocks, but you shouldn't nest it blocks because they won't work and only make a Christmas tree out of your code.

When you fire the npx wdio wdio.conf.js command, WebdriverIO searches the spec file's location in wdio.conf.js file's specs:[ ] parameter. It then loads all the available spec files in the path.

If you are from a Java Selenium background, the following syntax makes more sense to you. This is how single and multiple elements are traditionally located.

```
driver.findElement(By.LocatorStrategy("LocatorValue"));
  &
driver.findElements(By.LocatorStrategy("LocatorValue"));
```

These two statements can be written in WebdriverIO using $('selector') and $$('selector'), respectively. The catch is that you can only put CSS selectors and some specifics within single quotes, so an ID needs to be preceded by # and a class by a dot (.). This is discussed more later. Also, browser.url({ }) is a protocol binding to load the URL of the browser.

I used browser.pause command in Listing 2-1. The pause command ensures that the element is fully rendered in the Document Object Model (DOM) before taking a screenshot. The browser.pause command holds the WebdriverIO execution for a certain number of milliseconds, as specified in its argument. If you observe that the screenshots are not captured, blurry, or blank, you can tweak this parameter as per your Internet bandwidth or processing speed.

Now that you understand how Selenium locators are represented in WebdriverIO, let's look at the different types and the unique way WebdriverIO works with them. The following sections describe WebdriverIO supported locators (or selectors, as some call it).

ID

Refer to the example provided in Listing 2-1. #logo is the element ID that you took a screenshot of. Based on the World Wide Web Consortium(W3C), each element on a web page should have a unique ID. Although most dev guys don't follow this religiously, they do provide most elements with unique IDs, which makes this locator popular and reliable. Figure 2-5 is another example of locating an element by its ID, as shown in Listing 2-2. Make sure you comment out all other it blocks; otherwise, you see multiple results post-execution.

Syntax

```
$(#<idname>)
```

Listing 2-2. Finding an Element by ID

```
it('TC001.1_ID', () => {
    browser.url('https://www.saucedemo.com/')
    $('#user-name').saveScreenshot('Screenshots/TC001.1_ID.png')
})
```

Output

Username

Figure 2-5. Username fetched by ID locator

Class

The test case in Listing 2-3 opens a browser and navigates to the jQuery web site in the first line. The second line finds the element with the .project class and saves its screenshot. The .class selector selects elements with a specific class attribute. Multiple HTML elements are grouped as a class to achieve consistency in formatting. Figure 2-6 implies that the element was successfully located since a screenshot is saved. I use a screenshot as an example, however; you can do anything with the element once it's located, such as clicking text, which you will do in upcoming sections.

Syntax

```
$(.className) or $$(.className)
```

Listing 2-3. Finding an Element by Class

```
it('TC002_Class', () => {
    browser.url('https://jqueryui.com/')
    $('.projects').saveScreenshot('Screenshots/TC002_Class.png')
})
```

Output

Figure 2-6. *Output of the five icons that share the same class*

Notes

Make sure your folder structure in VS Code looks like Figure 2-7.

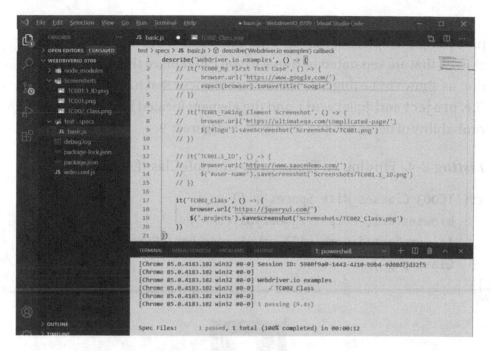

Figure 2-7. *State of framework structure*

You can comment out other it blocks except for the example you are currently working on, as shown in Figure 2-7. If you look closely at Figure 2-8, it has two classes—project and jquery-ui—separated by a space. Don't mistake them as a single class.

Figure 2-8. *A view of Google developer tools found by right-clicking the element and the Inspect element option*

Listing 2-3 identified a unique element with the .projects class in the preceding example, but that isn't the case most of the time. To handle classes that are separated by a space, you can replace the space with a dot, as shown in Listing 2-4. It shows an element that has both the class (i.e. project and jquery-ui), and the element located has a higher probability of being unique, as shown in Figure 2-9.

Listing 2-4. Finding an Element by multipleClass (AND)

```
it('TC003_Classes_With_Spaces', () => {
    browser.url('https://jqueryui.com/')
    $('.project.jquery-ui').saveScreenshot('Screenshots/TC003_
    Class.png')
})
```

Figure 2-9. *An icon with both project and jquery-ui classes*

If you need any elements that have the project class or the jquery-ui class, you can get it by placing a comma, like in Listing 2-5. Figure 2-10 shows Chrome's console when the .project.jquery-ui selector is used. The count returned by this selector is 6.

It returns multiple elements (i.e., an array of elements), which you handle with $$(") instead of $(") in Listing 2-5.

Listing 2-5. Finding an Element by multipleClass(OR)

```
it('TC003.1_Class_Count', () => {
    browser.url('https://jqueryui.com/')
    var multipleElems = $$('.project,.jquery-ui').length
    console.log(multipleElems)
})
```

The output is 6.

```
PROBLEMS    OUTPUT    DEBUG CONSOLE    TERMINAL         1: powershell        v    +   □   🗑   ∧   ×

[0-0] 6
[0-0] 2020-11-20T13:15:06.173Z INFO webdriver: COMMAND deleteSession()
2020-11-20T13:15:06.173Z INFO webdriver: [DELETE] http://localhost:9515/session/63af2a6e6667
082c8aef34b75496c4e1
[0-0] PASSED in chrome - F:\Automation\WebdriverIO_0709\test\specs\example.e2e.js
2020-11-20T13:15:06.410Z INFO @wdio/cli:launcher: Run onComplete hook

 "spec" Reporter:
------------------------------------------------------------------------------
[chrome 87.0.4280.66 windows #0-0] Spec: F:\Automation\WebdriverIO_0709\test\specs\example.e
2e.js
[chrome 87.0.4280.66 windows #0-0] Running: chrome (v87.0.4280.66) on windows
[chrome 87.0.4280.66 windows #0-0] Session ID: 63af2a6e6667082c8aef34b75496c4e1
[chrome 87.0.4280.66 windows #0-0]
[chrome 87.0.4280.66 windows #0-0] Webdriver.io examples
[chrome 87.0.4280.66 windows #0-0]    √ TC003.1_Class_Count
[chrome 87.0.4280.66 windows #0-0]
[chrome 87.0.4280.66 windows #0-0] 1 passing (3.6s)
```

Figure 2-10. *Output in terminal*

Instead of taking a screenshot, you fetched the element's count, since $$ always returns an array. The count is more appropriate in real-life scenarios. You applied the .length array method to get the number of elements in the DOM.

Name Attribute

The name attribute has the following elements: <a>, <applet>, <button>, <form>, <frame>, <iframe>, <img>, <input>, <map>, <meta>, <object>, <param>, <select>, and <textarea>. You do not find this attribute with <span> or <div>. To handle the former elements, you can use this locator strategy. Listing 2-6 uses the name attribute to find the Submit button locator. Figure 2-11 shows that the locator has successfully fetched the Submit button before taking the screenshot.

Syntax

```
$("[name = '<value>']")
```

Listing 2-6. Finding an Element by its Name Attribute

```
it('TC004_Name', () => {
    browser.url('https://ultimateqa.com/complicated-page/')
    $('[name="et_builder_submit_button"]').
    saveScreenshot('Screenshots/TC004.png')
})
```

Output

Figure 2-11. *Submit button located by name attribute*

Notes

Please be cautious using this locator strategy. According to official WebdriverIO documentation, this selector strategy is deprecated and only works in the old browser run on JSON wire protocol.

Tag Name

Sometimes you do not have attributes like ID, class, or name in an element, but elements like < td > tag or < tr > tag. In these cases, you can use the tag name locator strategy. I used the <img> tag in Listing 2-7 because it's the only <img> tag in the entire web site. This ensures that I get a unique locator, as shown in Figure 2-12.

Syntax

```
$('<tag>')
```

Listing 2-7. Finding an Element Using Its HTML Tag

```
it('TC005_TagName', () => {
    browser.url('https://www.saucedemo.com/')
    $('<img>').saveScreenshot('Screenshots/TC005_TagName.png')
})
```

Output

Figure 2-12. *Logo of a robot inside <img> tag identified by tag name locator*

Link Text

Hyperlinks are created with an anchor (`<a>`) tag and accompanied by linked text. If the anchor tag doesn't have a unique ID or name, you can use the link text locator strategy in Listing 2-8 to fetch the result, as shown in Figure 2-13.

Syntax

```
$('=anchorText')
```

Listing 2-8. Finding an Element Using Link Text

```
it('TC006_LinkText', () => {
    browser.url('https://ultimateqa.com/complicated-page/')
    $('=Courses').saveScreenshot('Screenshots/TC006_LinkText.png')
})
```

Output

Courses

Figure 2-13. *The output here is a link identified by link text locator*

Note

Listing 2-9 would make more sense in the real world if you use the click operation on the element, which you see in upcoming chapters. When there are two links with the same link text, this method only accesses the first one if you use $ instead of $$, which is confusing; so bear this in mind when using link text your locator strategy. In scenarios like this, it is advisable to use a different locator strategy for a more robust test script.

Partial Link Text

If the text is too long and you are confident it has a unique subtext that you can leverage to identify that element uniquely (like in Figure 2-14), you should use a partial link text locator strategy.

Syntax

```
$("*=<value>")
```

Listing 2-9. Finding an Element Using Partial Link Text

```
it('TC007_PartialLinkText', () => {
    browser.url('https://ultimateqa.com/complicated-page/')
    $('*=Random').saveScreenshot('Screenshots/TC007_
    PartialLinkText.png')
})
```

Output

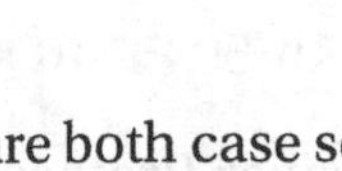

4 Section of
Random Stuff

Figure 2-14. *Output is a <p> tag with random subtext*

Note

Link text and partial link text are both case sensitive.

Elements with Certain Text

Certain text is one of the most useful locator strategies I have come across. I use it extensively, especially when testing react applications, as they contain a lot of <span> and <p> tags that do not have any attributes associated with them. Listing 2-10 shows how to find an element of the <span> tag comprising "Webdriver Protocol" text. If your screenshot for the following example seems blurry or incomplete when compared to Figure 2-15, try adding the pause command before the screenshot to pause the execution for 3 seconds (as shown in Listing 2-10) to allow the element to be completely rendered by the DOM. Similarly, an element with partial text in a <p> tag is captured in Listing 2-16.

Syntax

```
$('elementTag*=text')
```

Listing 2-10. Finding an Element with a Certain Text

```
it('TC008_Element With Certain Text', () => {
    browser.url('https://webdriver.io/docs/api.html')
    browser.pause(3000)
    $('span=Webdriver Protocol').saveScreenshot('Screenshots/
    TC008_CrtnTxt.png')
})
```

WEBDRIVER PROTOCOL

Figure 2-15. *Span text Webdriver Protocol button identified by element with certain text*

Finding an element by partial text is shown in Listing 2-11 and Figure 2-16.

Listing 2-11. Finding an Element with Partial Text

```
it('TC009_Element With Partial Text', () => {
    browser.url('https://ultimateqa.com/complicated-page/')
    $('p*=notifications').saveScreenshot('Screenshots/TC009_
    Partial.png')
})
```

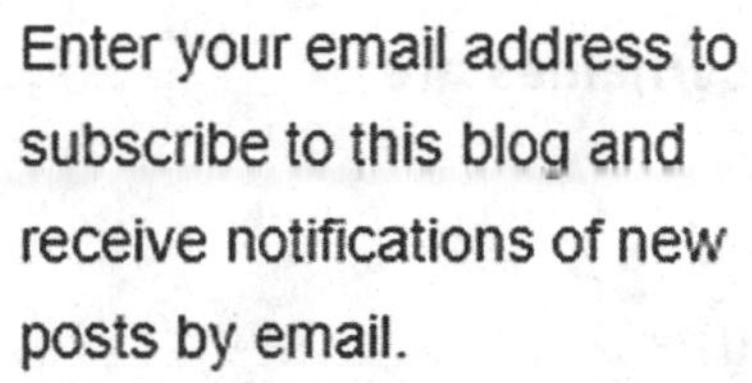

Enter your email address to subscribe to this blog and receive notifications of new posts by email.

Figure 2-16. *Text identified by element with partial text*

CSS Query Selector

If you cannot find elements with general locators like ID, class, and name, a CSS query selector is used, as in Listing 2-12. CSS selectors are a specific pattern through which you can uniquely locate an element in the DOM. CSS selectors select HTML elements according to their ID, class, type, and often a combination of them, as shown in Figure 2-17.

Syntax

```
$('CSS Query')
```

Listing 2-12. Finding an Element with Certain Text

```
it('TC010_CSSQuerySelector', () => {
    browser.url('https://www.saucedemo.com/')

$('div[class="login_credentials"]').
saveScreenshot('Screenshots/TC010_CSS.png')
})
```

Output

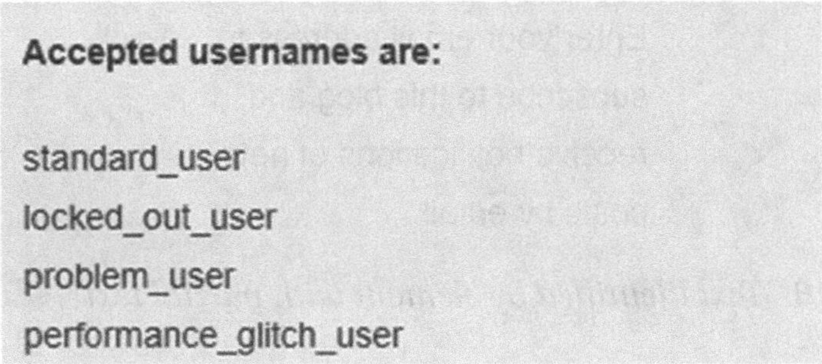

Accepted usernames are:

standard_user

locked_out_user

problem_user

performance_glitch_user

Figure 2-17. *Output is a div with class login_credentials*

Note

A little disclaimer: This CSS query selector fetched one element, which might not always be the case. You need to ensure that the selector you use fetches only the one element that you intend to target.

XPath

XPath is an XML path that navigates through the DOM of a web page. As you can see in Listing 2-13, it starts with a double slash. Although people claim that the XPath locator strategy is slower than a CSS selector, I have observed no great difference. Usually, people use either one of

these strategies based on familiarity and comfort or the strategy their
organization uses for test automation. The following code fetches the
Login button, as depicted in Figure 2-18.

Syntax

```
$('<starts with //>')
```

Listing 2-13. Finding an Element Through XPath

```
it('TC011_xpath', () => {
    browser.url('https://www.saucedemo.com/')
    $('//input[@id="login-button"]').
    saveScreenshot('Screenshots/TC011_xpath.png')
})
```

Output

LOGIN

Figure 2-18. *Login button identified by XPath*

Note

CSS query selectors are typically preferred more than XPath because
developers claim them to be faster in the long run, especially if you have
thousands of test scripts to run in a continuous integration environment.
Again, this is debatable. As a best practice, instead of keeping XPath as
your last locator strategy option, analyze other factors at play. You can ask
the developers to add ID to elements as much as possible, so you don't
have to always rely on XPath and CSS selectors.

To construct XPath, you can use the following syntax.

```
Xpath=//tagname[@attribute='value']
```

// selects the current node.

tagname is the node's tag name.

@ selects the attribute.

attribute is the node's attribute name.

value is the attribute's value.

Go to www.w3schools.com/xml/xpath_syntax.asp for more information on XPath.

JS Function

WebdriverIO gives you the flexibility of using vanilla JavaScript to fetch an element using web native APIs on the web page and return it successfully, as shown in Listing 2-14 and Figure 2-19, respectively.

Syntax

```
$(function() {return <JS script>})
```

Listing 2-14. Finding an Element Through JavaScript

```
it('TC012_JSFunction', () => {
    browser.url('https://ultimateqa.com/complicated-page/')
    $(() => document.getElementById('footer-bottom')).
    saveScreenshot('Screenshots/TC012.png')
})
```

Output

Figure 2-19. *Footer identified by JavaScript code*

Chain Selectors

You can't mix multiple selector strategies in one selector. However, you can filter your elements using multiple chained element queries to reach the same goal. Listing 2-15 finds an ID inside a form and only fetches an element name under the form div, as shown in Figure 2-20.

Syntax

```
$('selector').$('selector')
```

Listing 2-15. Chaining Locators

```
it('TC013_Chaining Selectors', () => {
    browser.url('https://ultimateqa.com/filling-out-forms/')

$('.et_pb_contact_form.clearfix').$('#et_pb_contact_name_0').
saveScreenshot('Screenshots/TC013_ChainSelectors.png')
})
```

Output

Name

Figure 2-20. *Element identified as a result of chaining locators*

35

Note

As soon as a locator is chained after another locator, its scope is confined to its predecessor's child elements. The web page may have numerous Submit buttons, but once it's chained after a div form, as shown in Figure 2-21, the locator only fetches one Button element inside the form.

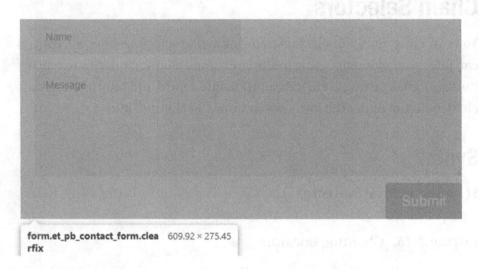

Figure 2-21. *Login button is inside a form element*

React Selectors

React is a front-end library for web development. React-generated locators are often dynamic; they change after each page refresh and are hard for traditional selectors to pin down.

Let's look at an example of React code that renders an element with a loginbutton ID. The following is a simple AppComponent instance inside the application, which React is rendering inside an HTML element with id="root".

Listing 2-16. Simple React AppComponent

```
// index.jsx
import React from 'react'
import ReactDOM from 'react-dom'

function AppComponent() {
    return (
        <div>
            AppComponent
        </div>
    )
}
function App() {
    return (<AppComponent />)
}
ReactDOM.render(<App />, document.querySelector('#root'))
```

Syntax

```
browser.react$()
```

Notes

The browser.react$ command allows you to select an instance of
AppComponent, which returns the WebdriverIO element for the first
<div/>, as shown in Listing 2-17.

Listing 2-17. Locating AppComponent

```
var appComp = browser.react$('AppComponent')
```

Refer to WebdriverIO documentation (https://webdriver.io/docs/
selectors.html#react-selectors) for more information on React selectors

Custom Selectors

You can create custom locators with JavaScript query selectors, similar to what you saw with the JS function selector. WebdriverIO converts the custom$() command to the executeScript() command to run a vanilla JavaScript query selector. Listing 2-18 defines the locator strategy with the addLocatorStrategy method to specify the query selector command that you want to use. In later steps, you call it via custom$(), which runs the query selector specified by the addLocatorStrategy method earlier in the code.

Syntax

```
browser.custom$(strategyName, strategyArguments)
```

Listing 2-18. Custom Locators

```
it("TC014_Custom Selectors", () => {
    browser.url("https://the-internet.herokuapp.com/")
    browser.addLocatorStrategy("ElemByCSS", selector => {
        return document.querySelectorAll(selector)
    })
    const elemByCSS = browser.custom$("ElemByCSS", "a[href*=
    '/abtest']")
    browser.pause(3000)
    elemByCSS.saveScreenshot('Screenshots/TC014_Custom.png')
})
```

Output

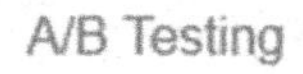

A/B Testing

Figure 2-22. *Custom locator identifies an element*

Notes

The `document.querySelector` and the `$()` methods let you locate and fetch an element from a web site's Document Object Model. However, each method has use cases. There are situations where Selenium alone can't identify web elements, but you can execute `javaScript(Custom$())` commands in Selenium. For instance, if the element is overshadowed by another element, or WebdriverIO finds it hard to click the buried element, it tries to mimic a real user's behavior during execution. If you want your code to force-click the element present in the DOM, use the `querySelector()` method, which uses vanilla JavaScript.

Summary

This chapter discussed strategies to uniquely locate elements. After identifying the elements, you captured their screenshots. In real life, this is only a small part of working with identified elements. There are many other operations, including simple functions like click, get text, and insert text, to more complex ones like drag-and-drop, selecting from drop-downs, and handling browser pop-ups. In the next chapter, you use WebdriverIO browser commands on locators to perform various functions.

CHAPTER 3

Browser APIs

Now that you have installed the WebdriverIO tool and learned how to locate an element in a web page, the next step is to develop a capability to perform actions on a located element. This chapter shows you how to perform various actions on a web page's located elements. You learn various commands to interact with elements, and you learn how WebdriverIO implements them with ease. This chapter covers the following.

- Debugging
- Simple tasks like
  - Clicking an element
  - Getting an element's text
  - Counting elements
- Complex tasks like
  - Dragging and dropping
  - Selecting from a drop-down
  - Switching between multiple windows

Browser APIs are built into your web browser and can expose data from the browser. WebdriverIO provides a set of easy-to-understand commands that wrap browser APIs to perform various browser tasks.

© Shashank Shukla 2021
S. Shukla, *Practical WebDriverIO*, https://doi.org/10.1007/978-1-4842-6661-8_3

Let's look at various activities that can be done on a web page and their respective WebdriverIO syntax and implementation.

Debugging

Before diving into the wonderful world of browser APIs, you need to understand how to debug a script. The `browser.debug()` command debugs test scripts. If you delete or comment out `browser.debug()` in Listing 3-1, the total time to execute these four lines of code is only a few seconds. This means you cannot check the application or a web page's state before the next command kicks in. In complex, animation-heavy web sites, you cannot know if the element you intended to click or work on is available at a specific instance during runtime. If available, is it in an active interactable state or not?

`browser.debug()` solves this problem. If you put this command before any step, it halts the execution and provides the opportunity to right-click and inspect the element to see its current state and the web page's overall state. When the execution is halted, you see the message shown in Figure 3-1 in your terminal.

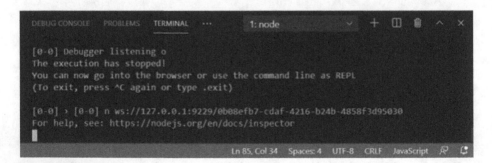

Figure 3-1. *Debug repl in the terminal*

Syntax

```
browser.debug()
```

Listing 3-1. Debugging WebdriverIO Code

```
it('TC015_Debugging the test case', () => {
    browser.url('https://www.google.com/')
    browser.debug()
    browser.url('https://en.wikipedia.org/')
    browser.debug()
    browser.url('https://webdriver.io/')
    browser.debug()
    browser.url('https://the-1nternet.herokuapp.com/')
})
```

Output

Although this test case does not have any output since it is simply navigating different web sites, you see the following logs for each web site visit.

```
INFO webdriver: COMMAND navigateTo("https://the-internet.
herokuapp.com/")
INFO webdriver: DATA { url: 'https://www.google.com/' }
[0-0] Debugger listen[0-0] ing on ws://127.0.0.1:9229/00c3db78-
3e85-4bbe-98a9-3075d40f18c8
For help, see: https://nodejs.org/en/docs/inspector

The execution has stopped!
(To exit, press ^C again or ^D or type .exit)
```

Notes

You applied multiple `browser.debug()` statements to achieve a step-by-step debugging experience; now you can resume the tests. Go to the terminal shell, use ^C (Control+C) twice or the `.exit` command to resume execution after each debug command.

You also need to change the timeout in the MochaOpts option in the wdio.conf.js file. Change it from 60000 (1 minute) to 6000000 (100 minutes), as shown in Figure 3-2, so your script does not timeout while you are busy debugging.

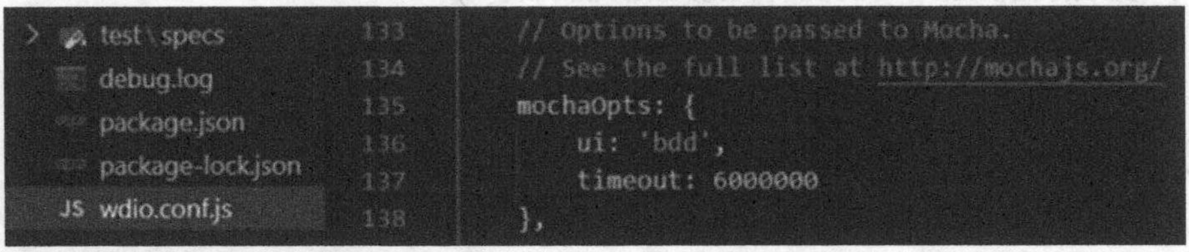

Figure 3-2. *Timeout settings in wdio.conf.js file*

Also revert the timeout to 1 minute (60000 ms) so that Mocha doesn't make you wait when your test case fails.

Loading URL and Basic Authentication

The `browser.url` function loads the URL once the browser starts. You can add authentication as part of this command. Basic authentication is a simple authentication scheme built into the HTTP protocol.

There is no specific API or command to automate basic authentication. If the web page requires you to authenticate, as shown in Figure 3-3, you need to place the username and password as part of the URL request in the username:password@url format (see Listing 3-2) to authenticate your request.

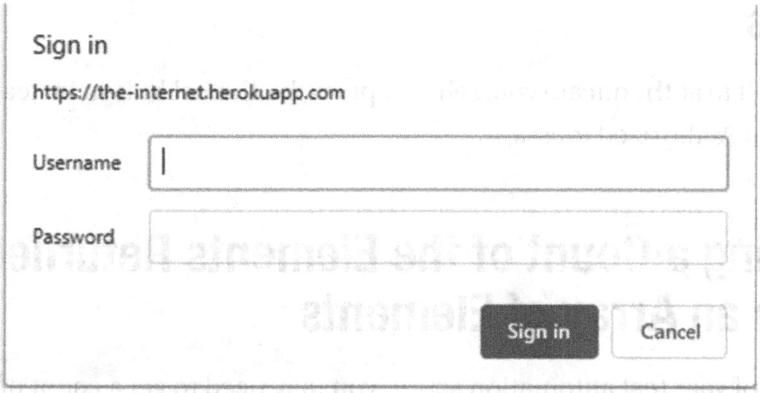

Figure 3-3. *Basic authentication pop-up in Chrome browser*

If your username and password are accepted in this instance, you see a message shown in Figure 3-4. It depends on the web site's coding.

Listing 3-2. *Augmenting the URL with userid and Password to Pass Basic Authentication Check*

```
it('TC016_Basic_Authentication', () => {
    browser.url('https://admin:admin@the-internet.herokuapp.
    com/basic_auth')
    browser.pause(3000)
})
```

Output

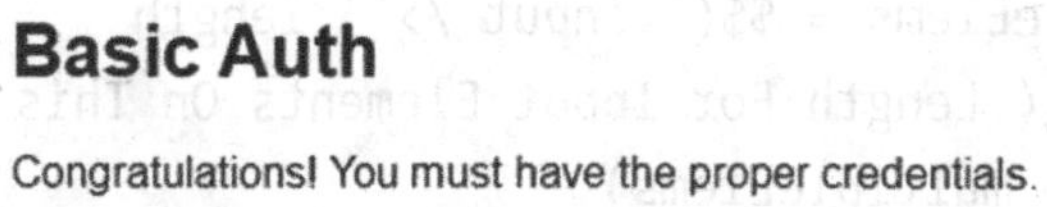

Basic Auth

Congratulations! You must have the proper credentials.

Figure 3-4. *Basic authentication successful message from the web site*

Notes

If you fail to authenticate yourself and press the Cancel button instead, you get a Not Authorized message.

Getting a Count of the Elements Returned from an Array of Elements

As part of your test automation script, you may need to get a count of the elements that you want to perform an action on. Sometimes you need to validate the number of elements present in the web page. In Listing 3-3, if you want to validate the total number of input fields present on a web page, you can use the `$$('selector').length` command and print it in the console via the `console.log` command. Use the `npx wdio wdio.conf.js` command to run this test case.

Syntax

`$$('selector').length`

Listing 3-3. Finding the Length Using JavaScript Array Length Function

```
it('TC017_length', () => {
    browser.url('https://www.saucedemo.com/')
    var multipleElems = $$('<input />').length
    console.log("Length For Input Elements On This
    Page :- " + multipleElems)
})
```

Output

```
Length For Input Elements On This Page is :- 3
```

Notes

Be advised that you cannot apply the array property (.length) to $('selector') because that always fetches a single element. Even when it identifies multiple elements, it can fetch only the first one.

Also, avoid placing a small bracket () after .length since Array. length is a property and not a function. The three elements identified by the input tag are the username, password, and the Submit button on the page in Figure 3-5.

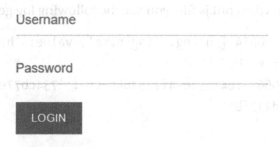

Figure 3-5. *The only three input tag elements in web page*

Getting the First Element Returned from an Array of Elements

$$(") returns an array of elements because it's a short way of calling the findElements command. And to get the first element of an array, you need to place [0] to specify the first index, as shown in Listing 3-4. WebdriverIO doesn't have a custom command to get the first element in an array. $$('selector') [0] is a vanilla JavaScript method, meaning that this method comes from a JavaScript/Node.js array ([ ])operator to fetch the elements in an array.

Syntax

```
$$('selector')[0]
```

Listing 3-4. Finding the First Element Fetched By $$ Selector

```
it('TC018_First_Element', () => {
    browser.url('https://the-internet.herokuapp.com/')
    var singleElem = $$('<h1>')[0]
    })
```

Output

You do not see any console output for this test; however, if your logLevel is set to `info` in the wdio.conf.js file, you see the following log generated.

```
INFO webdriver: DATA { using: 'tag name', value: 'h1' }
INFO webdriver: RESULT [{
    'element-6066-11e4-a52e-4f735466cecf': '734cb77e-51fb-4eff-
    9d4d-a3b50d211fbe'
  }]
```

Notes

A JavaScript array function can get any element by providing a relevant index ([ ]). In the preceding example, I demonstrate getting the first element with the first index (i.e., 0). It is common practice to get the element and do something with it (e.g., click it or get its text, which you see in upcoming examples). Here, I obtained the element and stored it in the `singleElem` variable; on its own, it is incomplete. Hence, if you print `singleElem` via console.log, you see the output as `[object Object]` because you are returning an object (element) as a string. Since there is no better vocabulary to represent an object as a string, the object's console.log value is set to "[object Object]" by the JavaScript engine. The next example brings it to a conclusion as you do something with this fetched element.

Getting the Text of an Element

The most logical step after successfully locating an element is to do something with it. In Listing 3-5, you get the text of the element located on the web page's menu bar, as shown in Figure 3-6.

Figure 3-6. *Web page menu bar*

Syntax

```
$('selector').getText() or $$('selector')[ '' ].getText()
```

Listing 3-5. Getting Text of the First Element Fetched from the Menu Bar

```
it('TC019_Get Text', () => {
    browser.url('https://jqueryui.com/')
    var elems = $$('.menu-item')
    var elem = elems[0]
    console.log("Text For First Menu Item:
    " + elem.getText())
})
```

Output

```
Text For First Menu Item: Demos
```

Notes

You can also write it directly, like console.log($$('.menu-item')[0].
getText()), but this limits you from reusing the element later in the test
case if you need to.

Getting the Text of any Element Returned from an Array of Elements

Let's try to get any of the eight elements' text in Listing 3-6. We'll use the
fourth element as an example. Reusing Listing 3-5, replace [0] from any
value between 0–7 and get the element you need from that array and
subsequently get its text via getText().

Syntax

```
$$('selector')[ 'n'].getText()
```

Listing 3-6. Getting Text of the Fourth Element Fetched from the
Menu Bar

```
it('TC020_Get Text', () => {
    browser.url('https://jqueryui.com/')
    var elems = $$('.menu-item')
    var elem = elems[3]
    console.log("Text For Fourth Menu Item:
    " + elem.getText())
})
```

Output

```
Text For Fourth Menu Item: Themes
```

Notes

Make sure you do not provide the index greater than the size of the array fetched by the locator; for example, var elem = elems[9] throws an error.

```
Cannot read property 'getText' of undefined.
```

Getting the Last Element Returned from an Array of Elements

Getting the last element is a little trickier than getting the first element or any element if you don't know what index the last element will be, which is almost always in real-world automation. You can find it by checking the length of an array first (line 4) and indexing the list of elements by (length -1) (i.e., the last element of the list shown in Listing 3-7).

Syntax

```
$$('selector')[length-1]
```

Listing 3-7. Getting Last Element Fetched from the Menu Bar

```
it('TC021_Get Last Element Of Array', () => {
    browser.url('https://jqueryui.com/')
    var elems = $$('.menu-item')
    var elem_last = elems[elems.length - 1]
    console.log("Text For Last Menu Item:
    " + elem_last.getText())
})
```

Output

Text For Last Menu Item: About

Iterating All Elements

You come across instances where you want to iterate through all the elements fetched by your locator. For example, clicking multiple fetched links or getting the text of multiple elements. Listing 3-8 shows how to get the text of all the elements you have identified by iterating them using the forEach method of the JavaScript arrays method. The forEach() method calls the function once for each array element. The function may perform any kind of operation on the given array elements.

Syntax

```
$$('selector').forEach(function(item){})
```

Listing 3-8. Iterating All Elements Fetched from the Menu Bar and Printing the Text

```
it('TC022_Get All Element Of Array', () => {
    browser.url('https://jqueryui.com/')
    var elems = $$('.menu-item')
    console.log('List of all items in Menu is: ')
    elems.forEach(function (item) {
        console.log(item.getText())
    })
})
```

Output

List of all items in Menu is:

Demo

Download

API

Documentation

Themes

Development

Support

Blog

About

Be advised that if you get some additional information between your test results as shown next, you can always turn it off by changing the parameter logLevel: 'info' to logLevel: 'silent' in the wdio.conf.js file.

```
[0-0] Download
INFO webdriver: COMMAND getElementText("1f294708-d8c6-4123-
aae2-89a4ec847b88")
INFO webdriver: [GET] http://localhost:9515/session/
fb54c30c9766e16298978f7b1a66713d/element/1f294708-d8c6-4123-
aae2-89a4ec847b88/text
INFO webdriver: RESULT API Documentation
[0-0] API Documentation
```

Notes

You are more likely to get a list of elements retrieved by selectors, such as class name, tag name, and CSS than name or ID, which usually only fetch a single element.

Getting All the Links on a Page

This is a favorite question of interviewers and probably a very good test to include in your regression suite. You can get all the page links using the getAttribute() method shown in Listing 3-9. Many other functions can be performed using forEach and getAttribute together, which I leave up to your creativity.

Syntax

```
$('selector').getAttribute(attributeName)
```

Code Snippet

Listing 3-9. Fetching All Links in the Web Page Through the Attribute of <a> Tag

```
it('TC023_Get All Links From Webpage', () => {
    browser.url('https://jqueryui.com/')
    var elems = $$('<a />')
    console.log('Links on the webpage are: ')
    elems.forEach(function (item) {
        console.log(item.getAttribute('href'))
    })
})
```

Output

Links on the webpage are:

> https://jquerymobile.com/
>
> https://sizzlejs.com/
>
> https://qunitjs.com/

.... You probably get a long list.

Notes

The same results are achieved using the Map function, which you see in the next example.

Map Function

The map() method creates a new array populated by calling a function on every element in the calling array. In Listing 3-10, you see how to achieve the same result using Map as you did previously by using forEach.

Syntax

```
$$('selector').map(function(){})
```

Listing 3-10. Fetching All Web Page Links Through Attribute of <a> Tag Using a Map Function

```
it('TC024_All Links From page via MAP', () => {
    browser.url('https://jqueryui.com/')
    var elems = $$('<a />')
    console.log('Links on the webpage are: ')
```

```
elems.map(function (item) {
    console.log(item.getAttribute('href'))
})
})
```

Output

Links on the webpage are:

https://jquerymobile.com/

https://sizzlejs.com/

https://qunitjs.com/

.... You get a long list.

Notes

You get the same result using .map as you do using forEach, but there is a subtle difference between them, as shown in Listing 3-11. The forEach() method doesn't return anything. It simply executes the function on each element of your array. However, map() returns an array of the same size. To simplify, forEach doesn't have to return the result of its operation in a new variable. In contrast, Map must explicitly return the result of its operation to a new variable.

Listing 3-11. Difference Between forEach and Map Function

forEach:
```
let arr = [1, 2, 3];
arr.forEach((number, index) => {
    return arr[index] = number * 3;
});
console.log("Returned Value of arr by foreach: " + arr)
```

Result:
```
// Returned Value of arr by foreach: 3,6,9
```
Map:
```
let arr = [1, 2, 3];
arr.map(num => {
    return num * 3;
});
console.log("Returned Value of arr by Map: " + arr)
```
Result:
```
// Returned Value of arr by Map: 1,2,3
```

In the preceding example, the arr array can be subjected to
.forEach() directly, but since map would return its result in a new variable,
you must store it in a variable, let's say *triple*, and print it, as shown in
Listing 3-12.

Listing 3-12. arr.map Result Returned as a Variable

```
let arr = [1, 2, 3];
var triple = arr.map(num => {
    return num * 3;
});
console.log("Returned Value: " + triple)
```

The result of this is *Returned Value: 3,6,9.* forEach can transform the
array it is applied to; however, Map cannot transform the array it is applied
to and has to provide its transformed array to a new variable. You can try
these out on your own in https://jsfiddle.net/ to get more clarity on
the concept.

Scrolling an Element into View

Selenium generally wants the element it is interacting with in view. To ensure your tests in WebdriverIO are more robust and less brittle, you need to interact with an element that is in eyesight by scrolling to that object on the web page.

Listing 3-13 visits The Internet web page (`https://the-internet.herokuapp.com`). Take a screenshot as soon as you land on the web page, and then scroll to the page footer and take a screenshot to compare.

Syntax

```
$('selector').scrollIntoView()
```

Listing 3-13. Scrolling into View

```
it('TC025_Scroll Into View', function () {
    browser.url('https://the-internet.herokuapp.com/')
    browser.saveScreenshot('Screenshots/TC024_BeforeScroll.png')
    $("#page-footer").scrollIntoView()
    browser.saveScreenshot('Screenshots/TC025_After Scroll.png')
})
```

Output

You find two screenshots saved in your project folder. The differences are apparent and self-explanatory.

Notes

$('selector').scrollIntoView() can be used for a horizontal or a vertical slider of an element fixed in the web site. They are usually embedded in the web site with the help of iframes, which you look at later in this chapter. You must first switch to that iframe before applying this method.

You can make the scroll smoother by using the command shown in Listing 3-14.

Listing 3-14. Scrolling to the Target Slowly

```
it('TC026_Scroll Into View_Slow', function () {
    browser.url('https://the-internet.herokuapp.com/')
    browser.saveScreenshot('Screenshots/TC024_BeforeScroll.png')
    $("#page-footer").scrollIntoView({ behavior: 'smooth'})
    browser.saveScreenshot('Screenshots/TC026_After Scroll.png')
})
```

If you get this error, then it most probably means the element is not in view, and you must scroll toward it to interact with it.

```
element not interactable
```

Click an Element

You can use the $('selector').click({ button, x, y }) command to automate mouse clicks in your test scripts, as shown in Listing 3-15. Automating click operations over elements on a web page is probably the simplest and most used operation.

Syntax

```
$('selector').click({ button, x, y })
```

Listing 3-15. Left-Click Function

```
it('TC027_Click', function () {
    browser.url('https://the-internet.herokuapp.com/add_remove_
    elements/')
    browser.debug()
    $('button=Add Element').click()
    browser.debug()
 })
```

Output

You do not see any output for this operation in the console; however, since you have applied two debug statements before and after the click() method, you observe the change as you resume the execution after both the steps. Clicking the Add Element button adds a new element in the DOM named Delete, which you see as the execution is paused by the last debug() method in your test script. The console produces WebdriverIO-generated logs, which you find behind the syntactical sugarcoating of the WebdriverIO command. It uses the WebDriver protocol's performAction class, which executes complex user actions for this activity.

```
INFO webdriver: COMMAND performActions(<object>)
```

Notes

Within the click function's round bracket, you can use one of the following options.

60

- `left` or 0 for left-click

- `middle` or 1 for middle-click

- `right` or 2 for right-click

If you leave it blank, it is a left-click by default.

In WebdriverIO, the default click function scrolls to the element before clicking it.

You can also use the provided x and y axis parameters to specify exactly where you want the click to happen. Listing 3-16 tries to send the second click exactly 80 pixels away from the original element. After some hits, I figured out it clicks the generated Delete button. If it doesn't work for you due to the difference in screen size, you can try changing the parameters.

Listing 3-16. Clicking Relative to the Object

```
it('TC028_Click', function () {
    browser.url('https://the-internet.herokuapp.com/
    add_remove_elements/')
    browser.debug()
    $('button=Add Element').click()
    browser.debug()
    $('button=Add Element').click({ x: 0, y: 80 })
    browser.debug()
})
```

Double-Click an Element

Sometimes you need to double-click an element (see Figure 3-7), which is done using the `$('selector').doubleClick()` command, as shown in Listing 3-17.

Demo:

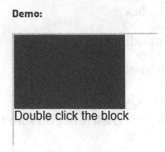

Double click the block

Figure 3-7. *A blue box that turns yellow when double-clicked*

Syntax

```
$('selector').doubleClick()
```

Listing 3-17. Double-Clicking an Element

```
it('TC029_Double Click', function () {
    browser.url('https://api.jquery.com/dblclick/')
    $('.demo.code-demo').scrollIntoView()
    browser.debug()
    browser.switchToFrame(0)
    $('<div />').doubleClick()
    browser.debug()
})
```

Output

If you use `browser.debug()` as suggested, you see a "The execution has stopped!" message. You can observe the block before and after the debug command by going to the browser.

You see the blue box turning into a yellow block once you resume your execution after the first debug command and complete the execution after the second debug command.

62

Notes

To show you the right example of double-clicking, I used this specific web site. Hence, two additional lines are added to the code to scroll into view and switch frames before double-clicking the element. Please ignore the switch frame for now and focus on the example's double-click behavior.

Right-Clicking an Element

You can also right-click an element using the click function parameters used in Listing 3-18.

Syntax

```
$('selector').click({button: 'right'})
```

Listing 3-18. Right-clicking an Element

```
it('TC030_Right_Click', () => {
    browser.url('https://www.saucedemo.com/')
    $('.bot_column').click({
        button: 'right'
    })
    browser.debug()
})
```

Output

There is no console output, but with `browser.debug()` in the last line, you hold the execution to observe the right-click menu items, as per your Windows settings.

Notes

You can also use button: 2 in line 4 of Listing 3-14. Be careful not to place it inside single quotes like this: '2'.

Sending Text to an Input Field

The $('selector').setValue("") command sends the text you want in the input field, as shown in Listing 3-19.

Syntax

```
$('selector').setValue("")
```

Listing 3-19. Setting "Search" of an <input> Tag

```
it('TC031_Set Value', () => {
    browser.url('https://jqueryui.com/')
    browser.debug()
    $('[name="s"]').saveScreenshot('Screenshots/TC028_before.png')
    $('[name="s"]').setValue("CSS Framework")
    browser.debug()
    $('[name="s"]').saveScreenshot('Screenshots/TC028_after.png')
})
```

Output

Please note that since you have applied debug, you must manually resume the testing, and you see the value change, as shown in Figure 3-8. Feel free to try it after removing the debug command.

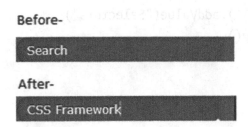

Figure 3-8. *Comparing before and after state of search bar*

Notes

It clears the existing value and then sends the text to the input field.

Sending a Text to an Input Field via addValue

$('selector').addValue(value) is another way to send the text to an input field. If the element value needs to be appended, you can use addValue, as shown in Listing 3-20.

Syntax

```
$('selector').addValue(value)
```

Listing 3-20. Adding Value "Selectors" After Setting Value "Search" in an <input> Tag

```
it('TC032_Add Value', () => {
    browser.url('https://jquery.com/')
    $('[name="s"]').setValue("Search")
    browser.debug()
```

```
    $('[name="s"]').addValue("Selectors")
    browser.debug()
})
```

Output

So if your input field has "Search", it adds "Selectors", making it "SearchSelectors", as depicted in Figure 3-9.

Figure 3-9. *Search bar of web site showing SearchSelectors as input*

Sending Keyboard Keys to an Element

The browser.keys() command is used when you must send special characters and keys like Esc, Enter, or Backspace, as shown in Listing 3-21.

Syntax

```
browser.keys()
```

Listing 3-21. Sending Three Backspaces After Sending the String "Selectors" to Get Final Result of "Select"

```
it('TC033_Keys', () => {
    browser.url('https://jquery.com/')
    $('[name="s"]').click()
```

```
    browser.keys("Selectors") //writes Selectors
    browser.debug()
    browser.keys("\uE003\uE003\uE003")
    browser.debug()
})
```

Output

Debug statements are applied so you can observe the execution. Line number 4 adds Selectors in the input field. Line number 6 removes ors (i.e., last three characters (uE003=backspace), and you are only left with Select.)

Notes

In Listing 3-21, you can send keystrokes like Esc, Shift, and Enter. It is necessary to click the element before using the Keys method.

Getting the Value of an Element

You can fetch the value of an input at any given instance with the getValue command, as shown in Listing 3-22.

Syntax

```
$('selector').getValue()
```

Listing 3-22. Fetching the Value of the Input Field and Printing It in the Console

```
it('TC034_Get Value', () => {
    browser.url('https://jquery.com/')
        $('[name="s"]').setValue("Selectors")
        console.log('Output is: ' + $('[name="s"]').getValue())
})
```

Output

Output is: Selectors

Notes

The difference between getValue() and getText() is that a get value fetches the input field's values in this case. However, getText only fetches blank.

Clearing the Text Inside an Input Field

As shown in Listing 3-23, the $('selector').clearValue() command clears the value entered in the input field.

Syntax

$('selector').clearValue()

Listing 3-23. Clears the Text in the Input Field

```
it('TC035_Clear Text', () => {
    browser.url('https://jquery.com/')
    $('[name="s"]').setValue("Selectors")
    browser.debug()
    $('[name="s"]').clearValue()
    browser.debug()
})
```

Output

The debug commands help you track the change in the Search field. No console output is expected for this test case.

Hovering the Mouse on an Element

The hover state refers to an element's properties when you mouse over it. Hover properties, such as a changing color or size, convey that whatever the mouse is over can be interacted with, as shown in Listing 3-24.

Syntax

```
$('selector').moveTo({ xOffset, yOffset })
```

Listing 3-24. End-to-End Test Case Featuring Mouse Hover Function

```
it('TC036_mouseMove', () => {
browser.url('https://opensource-demo.
orangehrmlive.com/')
$('#txtUsername').setValue("Admin")
$('#txtPassword').setValue("admin123")
```

```
                    $('#btnLogin').click()
                    $('#menu_admin_viewAdminModule').moveTo()
                    browser.pause(5000)
                    $('#menu_admin_UserManagement').moveTo()
                    browser.pause(5000)
                    $('#menu_admin_Organization').moveTo()
                    browser.pause(5000)
                    $('#menu_admin_viewCompanyStructure').moveTo()
                    browser.pause(5000)
                    $('#menu_admin_viewCompanyStructure').click()
                    browser.pause(5000)
        })
```

Output

No output in the console is expected, but if you are observant during the execution, you see the control hovering over the menu items, finally taking you to the Organization Structure section of the web site. Logs generated in the terminal explain that this command combines executeScript and the Actions class of the WebDriver protocol to achieve the task.

```
INFO webdriver: COMMAND executeScript("return { scrollX: this.
pageXOffset, scrollY: this.pageYOffset };", <object>)
INFO webdriver: COMMAND performActions(<object>)
```

Notes

I tried to include some of the earlier APIs covered in the MouseHover example as an end-to-end test for you. Here we have a web site in which you log in to the home page and hover over the Admin menu, which displays the Organization menu. Hovering over the Organization menu displays Company Structure, which you click .

Navigating to a New URL in a Browser

Command in Listing 3-25 navigates to a URL.

Syntax

```
browser.navigateTo(url)
```

Listing 3-25. Browser Navigating to `www.google.com`

```
it('TC037_Navigate', () => {
    browser.url('https://jqueryui.com/')
    console.log('First Website is : ' | browser.getTitle())
    browser.navigateTo('https://google.com')
    console.log('Second Website is : ' + browser.getTitle())
})
```

Output

```
First Website is : jQuery UI
Second Website is : Google
```

Notes

I used `browser.url('url')` and `browser.navigateTo('url')` in the same example, and you might be curious if you can interchange these. There is a difference between these two APIs. The `browser.url` method opens a URL, and it waits till the whole page gets loaded before returning control to the test or script. However, the `browser.navigate.to` method navigates to a URL and does not wait for the whole page to load. It maintains the browser history and cookies to use the forward and backward buttons to navigate the pages.

For more information, visit https://w3c.github.io/webdriver/#dfn-navigate-to.

You are introduced to the getTitle(), command, which displays the web page's title in the browser's title bar.

Navigating Back in a Browser

The browser.back() command navigates backward, as shown in Listing 3-26.

Syntax

```
browser.back()
```

Listing 3-26. Browser Navigating Backward

```
it('TC038_Back', () => {
    browser.url('https://jqueryui.com/')
    console.log('BasePage is ' + browser.getTitle())
    browser.navigateTo('https://google.com')
    console.log('Navigated to ' + browser.getTitle())
    browser.back()
    console.log('Navigated back to ' + browser.getTitle())
  })
```

Output

```
BasePage is jQuery UI
Navigated to Google
Navigated back to jQuery UI
```

Notes

You need to tread cautiously when using Back, because if there is no page in the cache to which the browser can go back to, it still passes your test script in Listing 3-27 and provides a blank title in the console.

Listing 3-27. Using back() Method Without Incorrectly

```
it('TC039_Back', () => {
    browser.url('https://jqueryui.com/')
    browser.back()
    console.log('Title is: '+ browser.getTitle())
})
```

Navigating Forward in a Browser

As shown in Listing 3-28, the browser.forward() command navigates forward.

Syntax

```
browser.forward()
```

Listing 3-28. Browser Navigating Forward

```
it('TC040_Forward', () => {
    browser.url('https://jqueryui.com/')
    console.log('BasePage is ' + browser.getTitle())
    browser.navigateTo('https://google.com')
    console.log('Navigated to ' + browser.getTitle())
    browser.back()
    console.log('Navigated back to ' +  browser.getTitle())
    browser.forward()
    console.log('Navigate forward to ' + browser.getTitle())
})
```

Output

```
BasePage is jQuery UI
Navigated to Google
Navigated back to jQuery UI
Navigate forward to Google
```

Refreshing a Web Page

You can refresh a page using the `browser.refresh()` command, as shown
in Listing 3-29. Alternatively, you can refresh a page by using an F5 keypress
in an input field on a page. In `$("s").Keys("\uE035")`, `\uE035` is F5.

You find all the supported Keys method characters at `https://w3c.`
`github.io/webdriver/#keyboard-actions`.

Syntax

```
browser.refresh()
```

Listing 3-29. Refreshing the Web Page

```
it('TC041_Refresh', () => {
    browser.url('https://the-internet.herokuapp.com/
    dynamic_content')
    browser.debug()
    browser.refresh()
    browser.debug()
})
```

Output

You see a visible difference in the web page's content before and after the refresh. I used the debug command in a scenario where the page changes on each refresh so you can observe it.

Notes

Keep in mind that when you interact with an element and refresh the page, the element becomes stale because it was destroyed and resurrected, giving you the following error.

```
Stale Element Reference Exception
```

The following is an excerpt from the official Selenium web site (www.selenium.dev).

> *The most frequent cause of Stale Element Reference Exception is that page that the element was part of has been refreshed, or the user has navigated away to another page. A less common, but still common cause is where a JS library has deleted an element and replaced it with one with the same ID or attributes.*

You need to use this cautiously when automating a web application. One solution is to locate the element and save it in a variable after the page refreshes to get a fresh reference of the element.

Restarting a Browser

The browser.reloadSession() command restarts a Selenium session, which in turn restarts the browser, as in Listing 3-30. It is useful when you want to clear a browser session, such as a browser cache between tests, especially when automating highly stateful web applications like

75

Facebook, Netflix, or any banking web site. Another use is when you want to test the login of an application with the "Remember me" checkbox checked, and then close the browser and open a fresh instance to see if the user is still logged in.

Syntax

```
browser.reloadSession()
```

Listing 3-30. Restarting the Browser

```
it('TC042_Reload Session', () => {
    browser.url('https://jqueryui.com/')
    console.log('session ID 1 = ' + browser.sessionId)
    browser.reloadSession()
    console.log('session ID 2 = ' + browser.sessionId)
})
```

Output

```
session ID 1 = cf51b0b0f386a8e4d44628934f291b19
session ID 2 = d64dcfd1392e682fcd61ceafb453367b
```

Getting and Setting Window Size and Position

Sometimes you must test your web application in a specific window size to see how the elements render on a tablet or a mobile phone. You can use the browser.getWindowRect() and browser.setWindowRect() commands, as shown in Listings 3-31 and 3-32, to get and set a specific browser window size and position.

Syntax

```
browser.getWindowRect()
browser.setWindowRect()
```

Listing 3-31. Get Browser Window Stats

```
it('TC043_Get Window Size', () => {
    browser.url('https://jqueryui.com/')
    console.log('Size & Position: ' + browser.getWindowRect())
})
```

Output of this depend upon your screen size. Hence, there is no absolute output for Listing 3-26.

For me it's- Size & Position: { height: 828, width: 1052, x: 9, y: 9 }

Listing 3-32. Set and Get Browser Window Using Different Parameters

```
it('TC044_Set Window Size', () => {
    browser.url('https://jqueryui.com/')

    console.log('Changing Window Position through X & Y axis')
    //x: 0, y: 0 i.e. Top Left
    browser.setWindowRect(0, 0, 400, 400)
    console.log(browser.getWindowRect())
    browser.pause(3000)
    //x: 0, y: 500 i.e. Bottom Left
    browser.setWindowRect(0, 500, 400, 400)
    console.log(browser.getWindowRect())
    browser.pause(3000)
```

```
//x: 500, y: 0 i.e. Top Right
browser.setWindowRect(500, 0, 400, 400)
console.log(browser.getWindowRect())
browser.pause(3000)
//x: 500, y: 500 i.e. Bottom Right
browser.setWindowRect(500, 500, 400, 400)
console.log(browser.getWindowRect())
browser.pause(3000)
console.log('Changing Window Size through height & Width-')
//height: 400, width: 400
browser.setWindowRect(0, 0, 400, 400)
console.log(browser.getWindowRect())
browser.pause(3000)
//height: 400, width: 800
browser.setWindowRect(0, 0, 400, 800)
console.log(browser.getWindowRect())
browser.pause(3000)
//height: 800, width: 400
browser.setWindowRect(0, 0, 800, 400)
console.log(browser.getWindowRect())
browser.pause(3000)
//height: 800, width: 800
browser.setWindowRect(0, 0, 800, 800)
console.log(browser.getWindowRect())
browser.pause(3000)
})
```

Output

Changing Window Position through X and Y axis

```
{ height: 400, width: 516, x: 0, y: 0 }
{ height: 400, width: 516, x: 0, y: 500 }
{ height: 400, width: 516, x: 500, y: 0 }
{ height: 400, width: 516, x: 500, y: 500 }
```

Changing Window Size through height and Width-

```
{ height: 400, width: 516, x: 0, y: 0 }
{ height: 800, width: 516, x: 0, y: 0 }
{ height: 400, width: 800, x: 0, y: 0 }
{ height: 800, width: 800, x: 0, y: 0 }
```

Notes

You can observe the outcome of this test on your screen to give you more idea on the changes in Window size and position by changing the parameters.

Getting Element Size

If you need to get the size of the element for validation, you can use the $('selector').getSize() command, as shown in Listing 3-33.

Syntax

```
$('selector').getSize()
```

Listing 3-33. Get Element Size

```
it('TC045_Get Element Size', () => {
    browser.url('https://jqueryui.com/')
    console.log('Logo Size: ' + $('.logo').getSize())
})
```

Output

Logo Size: { width: 243, height: 66 }

Notes

You can check the size of the web page by applying this to a body tag.

```
console.log($('<body />').getSize())
{ width: 912, height: 2119 }
```

Maximizing the Browser

The browser.maximizeWindow() command maximizes the browser according to your screen's dimensions. If your browser is not maximized before the WebdriverIO framework starts locating elements, all the elements in the web application may not be visible, resulting in a test failure. An element must be visible within the viewport for it to interact with Selenium.

It's also easier to view web pages and take screenshots on maximized browser windows. Listing 3-34 shows how to maximize your browser before the start of the test. Figure 3-10 shows the obvious differences in the viewport when the browser is maximized vs. when it's not, making it easier to find elements or take screenshots of the web page.

Syntax

```
browser.maximizeWindow()
```

Listing 3-34. Maximizing the Window

```
it('TC046_Maximize Window', () => {
    browser.url('https://the-internet.herokuapp.com/large')
    $('#header-1').scrollIntoView()
    browser.saveScreenshot('Screenshots/TC42_Before.png')
    browser.maximizeWindow()
    browser.saveScreenshot('Screenshots/TC42_after.png')
})
```

Output

Figure 3-10. *Difference in view port before and after maximize*

Notes

The best practice is to place this function right after the `browser.url` command in your test script, to increase the possibility of the element coming into the viewport and being located.

Minimizing the Browser

The browser can be minimized with the browser.minimizeWindow() command, as shown in Listing 3-35.

Syntax

```
browser.minimizeWindow()
```

Listing 3-35. Minimizing the Window

```
it('TC047_Minimize Window', () => {
    browser.url('https://www.google.com/')
    browser.pause(3000)
    browser.minimizeWindow()
    browser.pause(3000)
    browser.maximizeWindow()
    browser.pause(3000)
})
```

Output

There is no output, present in the console, but you need to observe the browser's behavior as the test is being executed to ensure the outcome is as expected. The browser should launch and stay the same size for 3 seconds. Then minimize it and remain that way for 3 seconds, and then maximize and stay maximized for 3 seconds before closing.

Notes

I cannot think of any scenario where a real-life user would want to minimize the browser as part of using a product or web app under testing; perhaps a test where the user has had a window minimized for quite some time and brings it back to focus to start interacting with your site. But ideally, it would not be a good candidate for automation.

Browser Fullscreen Mode

A browser can be made to work on a full screen with the browser. fullscreenWindow() command, as shown in Listing 3-36.

Syntax

```
browser.fullscreenWindow()
```

Listing 3-36. Fullscreen Window

```
it('TC048_Full Screen Window', () => {
    browser.url('https://jqueryui.com/')
    browser.fullscreenWindow()
    browser.pause(3000)
})
```

Output

No output in console; however, you need to be vigilant while the test is being executed. The Chrome browser enters full-screen mode for 3 seconds before shutting down.

Opening a New Window

Open a new tab in a browser as used in Listing 3-37. You can use the parameters provided by this function to open a window using specifics like in Listing 3-38.

Syntax

```
browser.newWindow({ options, windowName, windowFeatures })
```

Listing 3-37. Opens a New Tab

```
it('TC049_Open New Tab', () => {
    browser.url('https://jqueryui.com/')
    browser.newWindow('https://google.com')
    browser.pause(3000)
})
```

Listing 3-38. Opens a New Tab with Specific Parameters

```
it('TC050_Open New Tab with Specifications', () => {
    browser.url('https://jqueryui.com/')
    browser.newWindow(
        "https://google.com/",
        "Google",
        "width=200, height=400, resizable, scrollbars=yes"
    )
    browser.debug()
})
```

Output

Since your execution is paused by the last line of the `browser.debug()` code, you see a new tab open in the browser. If you have `logLevel` set as `info` in your config file (wdio.conf.js) file, you observe that behind the scenes, WebdriverIO calls the JavaScript `open()` function to archive the results.

```
script: 'return (function newWindow(url, windowName,
windowFeatures) {\n' + "    window.open(url, windowName ||
'new window', windowFeatures || '');\n" + '}).apply(null,
arguments)', args: ['https://google.com/', 'New Window', '']
}
```

Notes

You see how to switch to a newly opened tab and perform actions in an upcoming section.

Getting the URL of the Current Page

With the browser.getUrl()command, you get the URL for the page your control is presently in, as shown in Listing 3-39. This validates whether your navigation is correct before performing any further actions on the web page.

Syntax

```
browser.getUrl()
```

Listing 3-39. Get URL of the Current Web Page

```
it('TC051_GetURL', () => {
    browser.url('https://jqueryui.com/')
```

```
    const url = browser.getUrl()
    console.log('URL is: ' + url)
})
```

Output

URL is: https://jqueryui.com/

Sending JavaScript to do a Task: Vanilla JS Code

WebdriverIO can inject JavaScript and get its output back in the console for automation. Listing 3-40 doesn't particularly help with automation in the UI but injecting JavaScript as it is done in Listing 3-40 can help with multiple tasks during an actual execution. For instance, you can send Javascript to scroll down a page by certain number of pixels using window. scroll function.

Syntax

```
browser.executeScript()
```

Listing 3-40. Send JavaScript to a Web Page

```
it('TC052_Should inject javascript on the page', () => {
    browser.url('https://the-internet.herokuapp.com/')
    const result = browser.execute((a, b, c, d) => {
        return a + b + c + d
    }, 1, 2, 3, 4)
    console.log('Result is: ' + result)
})
```

Output

Result is: 10

Notes

The preceding example does not relate to automation testing; however, it shows the possibilities of what you can do by inserting JavaScript and jQuery in a page. Any functionality you can't find as a ready-made API in WebdriverIO can be done through `executeScript`.

JavaScript can perform the methods available in WebdriverIO. Like you can also send a click command using JavaScript. It's not ideal, but sending a click through JavaScript executer is an option. In Listing 3-41, `browser.execute()` has two arguments. One is the function, and the next one is the locator that needs to be worked upon by that function. You see the web site being navigated to Demos after continuing the execution.

Listing 3-41. Clicking an Element via JavaScript Snippet

```
it('TC053_Clicking', () => {
    browser.url('https://jqueryui.com/')
    browser.debug()
    browser.execute((elem) => {
        elem.click()
    }, $('=Demos'))
    browser.debug()
})
```

Sending JavaScript to do a Task: Handling Datepicker

You can use JavaScript to pick the date in the datepicker field, as shown in the Listing 3-42.

Syntax

```
browser.executeScript()
```

Listing 3-42. Date Picker

```
it('TCO54_DatePicker', () => {
    browser.url('https://jqueryui.com/datepicker/')
    browser.switchToFrame(0)
    //    $('#datepicker').click()
    browser.debug()
    browser.execute((elem) => {
        elem.value = '02/11/2019'
    }, $('#datepicker'))
    browser.debug()
})
```

Output

browser.debug() halts the execution before and after the step that fills in the date in the datepicker input element.

You see the following command in the console log. It sends user input to the input field with JavaScript's executeScript method.

```
INFO webdriver: COMMAND executeScript("return ((elem) => {
    elem.value = '02/11/2019'
}).apply(null, arguments)", <object>)
```

Notes

In the preceding code step 4 is an optional step, but it works both ways.

Taking a Full-Page Screenshot

The browser.saveScreenshot(filename) command in Listing 3-43 takes a fullscreen screenshot of the web page instead of a specific element.

Syntax

```
browser.saveScreenshot(filename)
```

Listing 3-43. Saving a Full Screen Screenshot

```
it('TC055_Full Screen Screenshot', () => {
    browser.url('https://jqueryui.com/')
    browser.saveScreenshot('Screenshots/TC055_Screenshot.png')
})
```

Output

You see a new .png file created under your project's Screenshots folder.

Notes

Be advised that it's not always a full-page snapshot. Depending on the browser, it only covers when the display viewport is visible to the user. Make sure that you adequately pause to let the page fully load before taking the screenshot.

Switching Between Windows

The browser.switchToWindow(handle) command switches the browsers' windows (tabs). If there is a link on the web page that opens in a new browser instance, you can use this command to transfer control over to the newly opened browser window and continue your automation journey of the test case (see Listing 3-44).

Syntax

```
browser.switchToWindow(handle)
```

Listing 3-44. Switch Between Window Tabs

```
it('TC056_Switch Betweeen Window by index match', () => {
    browser.url('https://webdriver.io')
    console.log('Base Window: ' + browser.getTitle())
    $('a[href="https://www.mozilla.org/"]').click()
    browser.pause(5000)
    let win = browser.getWindowHandles()
    browser.switchToWindow(win[1])
    console.log('New Window: ' + browser.getTitle())
})
```

Output

Base Window: WebdriverIO · Next-gen browser and mobile automation test framework for Node.js

New Window: Internet for people, not profit — Mozilla

Notes

`browser.getWindowHandles()` method is a prerequisite to `browser.switchToWindow()` method because it fetches the server assigned window handle numbers of all the open browser windows and save those as an array, in our case its variable 'win'. This allows us to switch to any open window using 'win' array variable and its respective index.

Switching Between Frames

Sometimes one web page is divided into many logical frames, where each frame can load its own separate HTML document. Frames organize a page into different zones. An inline frame, or iframe, is a part of HTML. It is a "box" that can be placed anywhere on your web site to embed documents or HTML bodies.

You cannot directly switch from one frame to another frame. You need to switch from the first frame to the main frame (with switchToParentFrame) and then from the main/parent frame to the second frame.

When there is a frame inside a frame, you need to go to the outer frame and then to the inner frame. Here, you don't need to go to the main frame (i.e., parent frame) first.

Listing 3-45 shows switching to an iframe to fetch the <p> tag, followed by fetching the <h3> header tag back at the parent web page.

Syntax

```
browser.switchToFrame()
```

Listing 3-45. Switch to a Frame

```
it('TC057_Switch between frames', () => {
    browser.url('https://the-internet.herokuapp.com/iframe')
    browser.pause(2000)
    browser.switchToFrame(0)
    console.log('Text inside frame: ' + $('<p>').getText())
    browser.switchToParentFrame()
    console.log('Webpage Heading on parent frame: ' +
    $('<h3>').getText())
})
```

Output

Text inside frame: Your content goes here.

Web page heading on parent frame: An iframe containing the TinyMCE WYSIWYG editor.

On closely watching the log details (logLevel: 'info'), you find how WebdriverIO transforms your commands to the WebDriver protocol that it uses to interact with the Selenium server and your browser.

```
COMMAND navigateTo("https://the-internet.herokuapp.com/iframe")
COMMAND switchToFrame(0)
COMMAND findElement("tag name", "p")
COMMAND getElementText("7e18fdfd-df4c-49d7-8a9a-754154da660a")
COMMAND switchToParentFrame()
COMMAND findElement("tag name", "h3")
COMMAND getElementText("8bcf02ec-d639-4ccf-a9bd-77d49f05d1fe")
COMMAND deleteSession()
```

And each of these commands has its corresponding Webdriver protocol commands, which are a little less user-friendly, as shown next.

```
[POST] http://localhost:9515/session/732eac666d2bac4aaed852f3f2
c341c8/url
[POST] http://localhost:9515/session/732eac666d2bac4aaed852f3f2
c341c8/frame
[POST] http://localhost:9515/session/732eac666d2bac4aaed852f3f2
c341c8/element
[GET] http://localhost:9515/session/732eac666d2bac4aaed852f3f2c
341c8/element/7e18fdfd-df4c-49d7-8a9a-754154da660a/text
[POST] http://localhost:9515/session/732eac666d2bac4aaed852f3f2
c341c8/frame/parent
[POST] http://localhost:9515/session/732eac666d2bac4aaed852f3f2
c341c8/element
```

```
[GET] http://localhost:9515/session/732eac666d2bac4aaed852f3f2c
341c8/element/8bcf02ec-d639-4ccf-a9bd-77d49f05d1fe/text
[DELETE] http://localhost:9515/session/732eac666d2bac4aaed852f3
f2c341c8
```

For more reference, please go to https://w3c.github.io/webdriver/

Notes

There are three ways to locate frames: name, locator, and index. The preceding example is the most common way of doing it (i.e., by index). We tried to get the editor's text inside a frame followed by getting the web page's heading.

The test fails if the switchToParentFrame command is not used because WebdriverIO searches the heading (<h3>) inside the frame rather than the whole web page. In this case, you get an error: "Can't call getText on element with selector "<h3>" because element wasn't found."

Closing the Page

As shown in Listing 3-46, the browser.closeWindow() command closes a browser tab.

Syntax

```
browser.closeWindow()
```

Listing 3-46. Closing a Browser Tab

```
it('TC058_Closing the tab', () => {
    browser.url('https://the-internet.herokuapp.com')
    browser.pause(1000)
    browser.newWindow('https://google.com')
    browser.pause(1000)
    browser.closeWindow()
 })
```

Output

Even though the output is not visible, your action generates a log in the console terminal.

```
INFO webdriver: COMMAND closeWindow()
INFO webdriver: [DELETE] http://localhost:9515/session/3953271f
83b9682a7b649756135952b5/window
```

It should not be confused with the browser shutdown command, which is automatically handled by WebdriverIO as follows.

```
INFO webdriver: COMMAND deleteSession()
2020-11-23T13:20:22.000Z INFO webdriver: [DELETE] http://
localhost:9515/session/3953271f83b9682a7b649756135952b5
```

Notes

If you close the tab where you started the instance from `browser.url`, everything closes—no matter how many windows are open. If you need to close a specific tab, you need to switch to it first and close it, as done in Listing 3-46.

Closing the Browser

The browser.deleteSession() command allows you to close the entire browser instance, as shown in Listing 3-47. This includes deleting the cookies.

Syntax

```
browser.deleteSession()
```

Listing 3-47. Delete Current Session of Selenium

```
it('TC059_Delete Session', () => {
    browser.url('https://the-internet.herokuapp.com/')
    browser.closeWindow()
    browser.deleteSession()
})
```

Output

```
INFO webdriver: COMMAND deleteSession()
INFO webdriver: [DELETE] http://localhost:9515/session/
d535f6ffdc7e25da517bbb89ea4cfbc6
```

Notes

It deletes the session. Be advised that for this example, `browser.close()` is not necessary before you delete the session. But sometimes it is necessary to close the browser before the test ends (typically, for the sake of mimicking real-life user interactions with the browser).

Alerts: Accepting an Alert

Developers use the alert() method to notify the user of something important. It displays an alert pop-up box with the intended message and an OK or Cancel button, as shown in Figure 3-11.

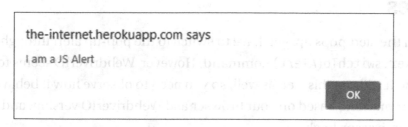

***Figure 3-11.** Alert box with OK as an option*

   The most common action required from the user is to accept the alert pop-up box by clicking the OK button, as shown in Listing 3-48. When the alert box pops up, it takes away the focus from the rest of the web site by making it inaccessible and forces the user to pay attention to the alert pop-up.

Syntax

```
browser.acceptAlert()
```

***Listing 3-48.** Accepting Alert*

```
it('TC060_Accept Alert', () => {
    browser.url('https://the-internet.herokuapp.com/javascript_
    alerts')
    $('button=Click for JS Confirm').click()
    browser.debug()
    browser.acceptAlert()
    browser.debug()
})
```

Output

Due to `browser.debug()`, the execution halts right before and after accepting the alert so you can observe the output.

Notes

When the alert pops up, you have to switch to the pop-up alert through the `browser.switchTo(Alert)` command. However, WebdriverIO seems to handle it without this step as well, so you need to observe how it behaves in your machine based on your browser and WebdriverIO version, and improvise accordingly.

Alerts: Dismissing an Alert

The next common alert action is to dismiss it by clicking Cancel, Dismiss, or any similar UI option provided in the web site template, as shown in Figure 3-12. A Dismiss option is available in a confirmation box, which can be automated, as shown in Listing 3-49.

Figure 3-12. *Confirmation box with OK and Cancel as options*

Syntax

```
browser.dismissAlert()
```

Listing 3-49. Dismissing an Alert

```
it('TC061_Dismiss Alert', () => {
    browser.url('https://the-internet.herokuapp.com/javascript_
    alerts')
    $('button=Click for JS Confirm').click()
    browser.debug()
    browser.dismissAlert()
    browser.debug()
      })
```

Output

Commonly, you do not notice the difference between accepting and rejecting an alert unless the web site is specifically programmed for it. You can verify this in your console. As opposed to acceptAlert in the previous example, dismissAlert logs the following in the terminal console.

```
INFO webdriver: COMMAND dismissAlert()
INFO webdriver: [POST] http://localhost:9515/session/52648d6965
08320eddd967cd17d1ba2d/alert/dismiss
```

Notes

A confirmation box looks like an alert box, but it uses the confirm("message") function as opposed to an alert box, which uses an alert("message") function, and therefore has an additional option for cancellation.

Alerts: Sending a Message to an Alert

There is another type of pop-up box used in JavaScript called a *prompt box*, as shown in Figure 3-13. It takes user input. After entering the input, the user must click OK to proceed, as shown in Listing 3-50, to get the final output (see Figure 3-14).

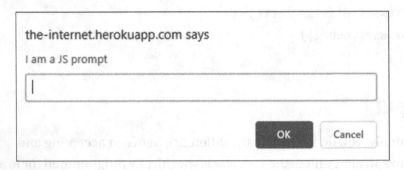

Figure 3-13. Prompt box with input field

The user can also click the Cancel button, which returns a null value.

Syntax

```
browser.sendAlertText()
```

Listing 3-50. Sending Text from An Alert

```
it('TC062_Send Message to Alert', () => {
    browser.url('https://the-internet.herokuapp.com/javascript_
    alerts')
    $('button=Click for JS Prompt').click()
    browser.pause(2000)
    browser.sendAlertText('WebdriverIO is Awesome!!!')
    browser.acceptAlert();
```

```
browser.pause(5000)
browser.saveScreenshot('Screenshots/TC062_sendAlertText.png')
})
```

Output

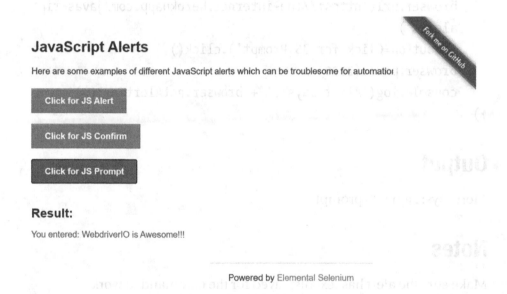

JavaScript Alerts

Here are some examples of different JavaScript alerts which can be troublesome for automation

Click for JS Alert

Click for JS Confirm

Click for JS Prompt

Result:

You entered: WebdriverIO is Awesome!!!

Powered by Elemental Selenium

Figure 3-14. *Input captured from alert is displayed*

Notes

Developers use `prompt("message")` in coding when they require a prompt box to get the users' input.

Alerts: Reading an Alert Message

You can fetch an alert's text by using the browser.getAlertText() command, as shown as Listing 3-51.

Syntax

```
browser.getAlertText()
```

Listing 3-51. Reading Text from an Alert

```
it('TC062_Read Message from Alert', () => {
    browser.url('https://the-internet.herokuapp.com/javascript_
    alerts')
    $('button=Click for JS Prompt').click()
    browser.pause(2000)
    console.log('Alert says: ' + browser.getAlertText())
})
```

Output

Alert says: I am a JS prompt

Notes

Make sure the alert has text displayed for the command to work.

Selecting from a Drop-Down

Drop-downs allow the user to choose one value from a list. It displays (drops down) a list of options, from which the user can select one. User actions on a drop-down can be automated in three ways: selecting an option by its attribute value, as shown in Listing 3-52; selecting an option by its index, as shown in Listing 3-53; or selecting an option by its visible text, as shown in Listing 3-54.

Syntax

```
browser.selectByAttribute()
browser.selectByIndex()
browser.selectByVisibleText()
```

Listing 3-52. Selecting a Relevant Option from Drop-Down by Matching Attribute Value

```
it('TC063_Select dropdown by "Attribute"', () => {
    browser.url('https://the-internet.herokuapp.com/dropdown')
    browser.pause(2000)
    $('#dropdown').selectByAttribute('value', '1')
    browser.debug()
})
```

Listing 3-53. Selecting a Relevant Option from Drop-Down by Matching Index

```
it('TC064_Select dropdown by "Index"', () => {
    browser.url('https://the-internet.herokuapp.com/dropdown')
    browser.pause(2000)
    $('#dropdown').selectByIndex(2)
    browser.debug()
})
```

Listing 3-54. Selecting a Relevant Option from Drop-Down by Matching Visible Text

```
it('TC065_Select dropdown by "Visible Text"', () => {
    browser.url('https://the-internet.herokuapp.com/dropdown')
    browser.pause(2000)
    $('#dropdown').selectByVisibleText('Option 1')
    browser.debug()
})
```

Output

You observed all the three ways to select from a drop-down in the preceding listings. The outcome is the same, which can be observed from UI if you notice that the command was converted to the `findElementFromElement` WebDriver protocol command. This is the same command used by the WebdriverIO `$().$()` chained locator that you saw in Chapter 2. As soon as a locator is chained after another locator, its scope is confined to its predecessor's child elements.

`browser.findElementFromElement(elementId, using, value)` takes in three arguments: the element ID of the parent under which the child element should be found, the locator strategy for how the child element should be found, and the value of the locator strategy. In the following logs, it tries to find it using XPath and CSS selectors.

```
INFO webdriver: COMMAND findElementFromElement("8e07fc42-11b9-
4400-8f63-eb048e28dcc2", "xpath", "./option[normalize-space(
@value) = "1"]|./optgroup/option[normalize-space(@value) = "1"]")

INFO webdriver: COMMAND findElementsFromElement("7de2378a-661b-
4ec8-b54b-c75eee9c8e61", "css selector", "option")
```

```
INFO webdriver: COMMAND findElementFromElement("cf438ead-
8b8c-46ef-b2e6-8d41b2b76ebe", "xpath", "./option[. = "Option
1"]|./option[normalize-space(text()) = "Option 1"]|./
optgroup/option[. = "Option 1"]|./optgroup/option[normalize-
space(text()) = "Option 1"]")
```

Drag and Drop

Dragging and dropping seems complex, but with WebdriverIO, you need a source locator and a target locator. Listing 3-55 has one line of code to drag an element and drop it into its target location.

Syntax

```
$('selector').dragAndDrop('selector')
```

Listing 3-55. Dragging and Dropping an Element from Source to Target

```
it('TC066_Drag & Drop', () => {
    browser.url('https://jqueryui.com/resources/demos/
    droppable/default.html')
    browser.pause(1000)
    $('#draggable').dragAndDrop($('#droppable'))
    browser.debug()
      })
```

Output

When your execution halts, you see the results shown in Figure 3-15.

105

Drag me to
my target

Figure 3-15. *Drag-and-drop action completed*

When closely observing console logs, you see that in the background, WebdriverIO breaks down its simple drag-and-drop command to multiple individual commands required to interact with the Selenium server and the browser.

```
COMMAND executeScript("return { scrollX: this.pageXOffset,
scrollY: this.pageYOffset };", <object>)
COMMAND getElementRect("a503b8fc-144d-48ca-a60f-8d6e54e0fab2")
COMMAND getElementRect("d9768513-cad7-44b6-a088-f4594a12b22a")
COMMAND performActions(<object>)
COMMAND releaseActions()
```

Notes

You can also drag and drop a source relative to its position through the $('#draggable').dragAndDrop({ x: 100, y: 100 }) command, where the element is dropped relative to its position.

Uploading a File

Some web pages need to upload files, as shown in Figure 3-16. There is no separate API to upload a file. You only need to ensure the field is an HTML tag input type and use the addValue command to provide the file's absolute path. Click the Submit button, as in Listing 3-56, and you get a success message, as shown in Figure 3-17.

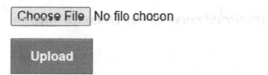

Figure 3-16. *Form with file upload as an option*

Listing 3-56. Uploading a File

```
it('TC067_File Upload', () => {
    browser.url('https://the-internet.herokuapp.com/upload')
    $('#file-upload').addValue('Z:/Automation/TC001.png')
    $('#file-submit').click()
    browser.debug()
})
```

Output

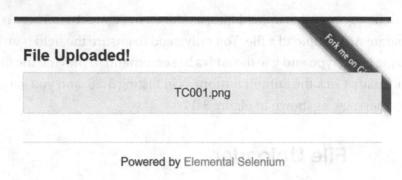

Figure 3-17. *File uploaded successfully UI confirmation*

Notes

You need to ensure that you use your own file's absolute path in your system since the code won't work exactly as provided in Listing 3-56.

Submitting a Form
Notes

`browser.submitForm('selector')` was depreciated after WebdriverIO version 4. You must either click the Submit button or press the Enter key via the `browser.keys()` command.

Display Cookies

Cookies are small bits of data stored as plain text files on your computer through the web site browser. Cookies can be displayed using the `browser. getCookies()` command, as shown in Listing 3-57.

Syntax

```
browser.getCookies()
```

Listing 3-57. Getting All Cookies and Getting a Cooking By Its Name

```
it('TCO68_Get Cookies', () => {
    browser.url('https://the-internet.herokuapp.com/')
    console.log(browser.getCookies()) //all cookies
    console.log("/////////////////////////")
    console.log(browser.getCookies(['optimizelyBuckets']))
    //specific cookies
})
```

Output

```
[0-0] /////////////////////////
[
  {
    name: 'optimizelyBuckets',
    value: '%7B%7D',
    domain: '.the-internet.herokuapp.com',
    path: '/',
    expires: 1917168566,
    size: 23,
    httpOnly: false,
    secure: false,
    session: false
  }
]
```

Notes

I removed the .getCookies() results because it was too long. You see how to get a cookie by its name; in this case, 'optimizelyBuckets'.

Delete Cookies

Cookies can be deleted by using the browser.deleteCookies()command, as shown in Listing 3-58.

Syntax

```
browser.deleteCookies()
```

Listing 3-58. Getting All Cookies and Deleting a Cooking By Its Name

```
it('TC069_Delete Cookies', () => {
    browser.url(' https://the-internet.herokuapp.com/')
    console.log(browser.getCookies()) //gets all cookies
    console.log("//////////////////////////")
    browser.deleteCookies(['optimizelyBuckets'])
    console.log(browser.getCookies())
 })
```

Output

In the console logs, you see all cookies except 'optimizelyBuckets' because it was deleted.

Notes

If you don't provide a parameter for deleteCookies, it deletes all cookies.

Set Cookies

You can add custom cookies during your execution by using the browser. setCookies() command, as shown in Listing 3-59.

Syntax

```
browser.setCookies()
```

Listing 3-59. Setting Cookies with Specific Values

```
it('TC070_Set Cookies', () => {
    browser.url(' https://the-internet.herokuapp.com/')
    console.log(browser.getCookies()) //gets all cookies
    browser.setCookies([ //adds specefic cookies
        {
            name: 'test2',
            value: 'two'
        },
        {
            name: 'test3',
            value: 'three'
        }
    ])
    console.log("/////////////////////////")
    console.log(browser.getCookies())
})
```

Output

```
////////////////////////
[
  {
    name: 'test3',
    value: 'three',
    domain: 'the-internet.herokuapp.com',
    path: '/',
    expires: -1,
    size: 10,
    httpOnly: false,
    secure: true,
    session: true
  },
  {
    name: 'test2',
    value: 'two',
    domain: 'the-internet.herokuapp.com',
    path: '/',
    expires: -1,
    size: 8,
    httpOnly: false,
    secure: true,
    session: true
  },
```

Notes

You see other cookies, which I removed from the output.

Geolocations

Geolocation refers to a browser identifying a user's or a computing device's geographic location via various data collection mechanisms, as shown in Figure 3-18.

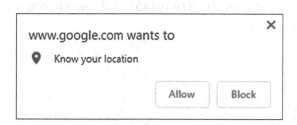

Figure 3-18. Geolocation permission request in Chrome

In some scenarios, you need to automate tests related to a specific location; for instance, automating a test from India to find the branches of a bank located in the United States. Listing 3-60 shows how to override and fake geolocations according to your automation test case requirements.

You need to complete the following prerequisites to run the geolocations script: install devtools-service and add devtools in the services field in config.js file, as `services: ['devtools']`.

```
Dependency-
npm install @wdio/devtools-service --save-dev
```

```
In config file-
  services: ['devtools'],
```

Depending on your browser version, Chrome may be unable to handle the permissions pop-up shown in Figure 3-18. Thus, you need to work around it manually by clicking the pop-up during the execution to get the desired output in the UI, as shown in Figure 3-19. The resolution of this manual workaround depends on your WebdriverIO and browser versions. I advise you to search for a resolution online, and if there is a suggestion to upgrade your WebdriverIO version, park this example until you have run all other examples.

You can refer to the open query on Stack Overflow at https:// stackoverflow.com/questions/64944620/allow-chrome-geolocation- popup-in-webdriverio.

Syntax

```
browser.cdp()
```

Listing 3-60. Setting Geolocation Somewhere Around Bermuda Triangle via CDP

```
it('TC071_Geolocations', () => {
    browser.url('https://whatmylocation.com/')
    browser.cdp('Emulation', 'setGeolocationOverride', {
        latitude: 40.758896,
        longitude: -73.985130,
        accuracy: 1
    })
    browser.cdp('Emulation', 'setTimezoneOverride', {
        timezoneId: 'Europe/London'
    })
    browser.pause(5000)
    $('#mapholder').saveScreenshot('Screenshots/TC071_map.png')
})
```

Output

You're here at:
1553 Broadway, New York, NY 10036-1517, United States

Figure 3-19. *Map captured from a div locator*

Notes

Don't forget to revert the services setting changes in wdio.conf.js back to services: ['chromedriver'] once the test case completes.

Summary

After trying out these examples yourself, I am sure you better understand the WebdriverIO tool's workings and capabilities. There are thousands of possibilities for automating an end-to-end flow. Once you know the fundamentals, you can start exploring and experimenting with different browser commands and build upon your existing knowledge to automate highly complex tests.

Now that you've learned about installation, locators, and APIs, let's look at other element-specific APIs provided by WebdriverIO.

CHAPTER 4

Element APIs and WebdriverIO Assertions

In the previous chapter, you learned about browser-specific APIs. This chapter discusses element-specific APIs. You use various assertions provided natively by WebdriverIO. Broadly, this chapter covers the following topics.

- APIs and assertions

- Presence or absence of elements

- Selected and unselected elements

- Displayed or hidden elements

- Enabled and disabled elements

- Clickable and unclickable elements

WebdriverIO element APIs and assertions have one basic difference. Element APIs/commands return *true* or *false* values. You can use a value to validate a test flow. An assertion doesn't return true or false but halts the execution to let you know if the validation passed or failed. You can

© Shashank Shukla 2021
S. Shukla, *Practical WebDriverIO*, https://doi.org/10.1007/978-1-4842-6661-8_4

throw in various element APIs in a test case, but only the assertion should determine if your test passes or fails. Let's look at this with examples to get a better idea. First, create a new .js file in the project to segregate the examples based on chapters.

Is the Element Present?: isExisting()

You can get an element's status with the isElement() method. Figure 4-1 shows a web page that dynamically loads an element after few seconds. When you click the Start button, the element (a <p> tag, Hello World!) renders after few seconds, as depicted in Figure 4-2.

The test in Listing 4-1 first loads the URL and then clicks the Start button, immediately printing the status of the <p> tag element using the isExisting() element API. It then waits for 10 seconds and prints the status again.

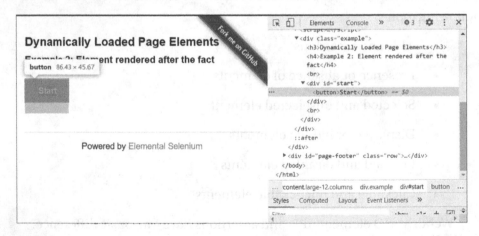

Figure 4-1. *Start button in the web page*

Syntax

```
isExisting()
```

Listing 4-1. Element API isExisitng()

```
it('TC071_isExisting()', () => {
    browser.url('https://the-internet.herokuapp.com/dynamic_
    loading/2')
    var elem = $('#finish')
    $('button=Start').click()
    console.log('Existence of element after Start button is
    clicked= ')
    console.log(elem.isExisting())
    browser.pause(10000)
    var elem = $('#finish')
    console.log('Existence of element after a 10 second pause= ')
    console.log(elem.isExisting())
})
```

Output

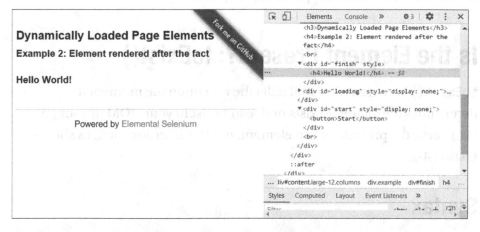

Figure 4-2. *Hello World! present in the web page*

Since the element renders after 10 seconds during the second attempt, the command returns true in the second attempt as opposed to a false in the first attempt, as shown in Figure 4-3.

```
[0-0] Existence of element after Start button is clicked=
[0-0] false
[0-0] Existence of element after a 10 second pause=
[0-0] true
[0-0] PASSED in chrome - F:\Automation\WebdriverIO_0709\test\specs\basic.js
```

Figure 4-3. *Console log in the terminal*

Notes

This is an element API and not an assertion, which means your test in Listing 4-1 will not fail, even if your locator doesn't find the element in the DOM.

During the execution, the element renders well ahead of a 10-second pause. A hard 10-second pause is not a good practice. You learn more about intelligent waits in upcoming chapters.

Is the Element Present?: toExist()

toExist() is an assertion that halts the execution the moment it determines the element exists or doesn't exist in your DOM. If your goal is to verify the presence of an element, use the assertion for it, as shown in Listing 4-2.

Syntax

toExist()

Listing 4-2. toExist() Assertion

```
it('TC072_toExist()', () => {
    browser.url('https://the-internet.herokuapp.com/
    dynamic_loading/2')
    var elem = $('#finish')
    expect(elem).toExist()
    $('button=Start').click() //won't get executed
    browser.pause(10000) //won't get executed
    expect(elem).toExist() //won't get executed
})
```

Output

```
Spec Files:        0 passed, 1 failed, 1 total (100% completed)
in 00:00:21
```

```
Error: Expect $(`#finish`) to exist

Expected: "exist"
Received: "not exist"
```

Figure 4-4. *Console showing a failed assertion in terminal output*

Notes

You can use the isExisting() element API and work your way forward
after receiving its true or false return value (status). In Listing 4-2, the
last three lines of code do not execute because they are placed after the
assertion for demonstration purposes.

Is the Element Present?: toBePresent()

toBePresent() is an assertion. It is the same as toExist(), but you can choose either of them, depending on whichever suits your team.

Listing 4-3 shows toBePresent() used in the same code. You can compare the output differences in Figure 4-5.

Syntax

toBePresent()

Listing 4-3. toBePresent() Assertion

```
it('TC073_toBePresent()', () => {
    browser.url('https://the-internet.herokuapp.com/
    dynamic_loading/2')
    var elem = $('#finish')
    expect(elem).toBePresent()
    $('button=Start').click() //won't get executed
    browser.pause(10000) //won't get executed
    expect(elem).toBePresent() //won't get executed
 })
```

Output

```
Spec Files:      0 passed, 1 failed, 1 total (100% completed)
in 00:00:24
```

```
[chrome 87.0.4280.66 windows #0-0] Expect $(`#finish`) to be present

Expected: "present"
Received: "not present"
```

Figure 4-5. *Console showing a failed assertion in terminal output*

Note

The workings are similar to toExist().

Is the Element Present in DOM?: ToBeExisting()

toBeExisting() is an assertion API that is the same as toExist() and toBePresent(), as shown in Listing 4-4.

Syntax

toBeExisting()

Listing 4-4. toBeExisting() Assertion

```
it('TC074_toBeExisting()', () => {
    browser.url('https://the-internet.herokuapp.com/
    dynamic_loading/2')
    var elem = $('#finish')
    expect(elem).toBeExisting()
    $('button=Start').click() //won't get executed
    browser.pause(10000) //won't get executed
    expect(elem).toBeExisting() //won't get executed
})
```

123

Output

```
Spec Files:       0 passed, 1 failed, 1 total (100% completed)
in 00:00:23
```

```
[chrome 87.0.4280.66 windows #0-0] Expect $( #finish ) to be existing

Expected: "existing"
Received: "not existing"
```

Figure 4-6. *Console showing a failed assertion in terminal output*

Notes

Whether you use toExist(), BePresent(), or toBeExisting(), ensure that is consistent across your automation suite.

Is the Element Enabled?: IsEnabled()

Figure 4-7 shows a grayed-out textbox, which means that it is disabled. Web developers can enable or disabled certain element tags by modifying an element property disabled in HTML code <input type="text" disabled="disabled" />. This is primarily used for elements like radio buttons and input fields. You can check if an element is enabled or disabled by using the isEnabled() method.

Listing 4-5 navigates to the URL and identifies the disabled input text field. Next, the isEnabled() method prints the field's status before clicking the Enable button. The next step clicks the Enable button in the UI, which applies the isEnabled() method after 5 seconds to print the result. The output is shown in Figure 4-8. The first isEnabled() method returns false but returns true the second time.

If you apply browser.debug in the last step and inspect the input element, you can see the difference, as shown in Figure 4-9.

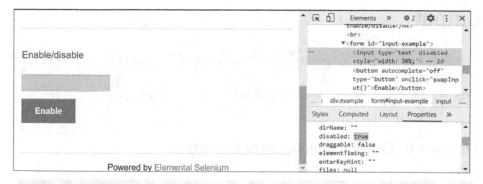

Figure 4-7. *Disabled text box*

Syntax

isEnabled()

Listing 4-5. isEnabled() Element API

```
it('TCO75_isEnabled()', () => {
    browser.url('https://the-internet.herokuapp.com/
    dynamic_controls')
    var elem = $('input[type="text"]')
    console.log('Verifying element is Enabled before clicking
    button=')
    console.log(elem.isEnabled())
    $('button=Enable').click()
    browser.pause(5000)
    var elem = $('input[type="text"]')
    console.log('Verifying element is Enabled after clicking
    button= ')
    console.log(elem.isEnabled ())
    browser.debug()
})
```

Output

```
[0-0] Verifying element is Enabled before clicking button=
[0-0] false
[0-0] Verifying element is Enabled after clicking button=
[0-0] true
```

Figure 4-8. *Console showing terminal output*

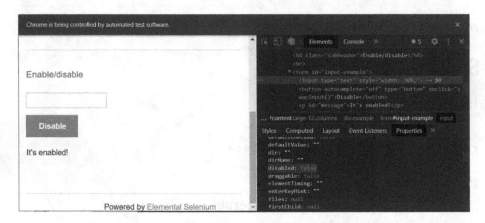

Figure 4-9. *Difference in <input> tag HTML code after Enable button is clicked*

Notes

isEnabled() checks for the disabled attribute in a property. If the button is disabled by any other means, isEnabled() might not work.

Is the Element Enabled?: toBeEnabled()

toBeEnabled() is an assertion. Therefore, it passes or fails the test case depending on the element's status as true or false. Listing 4-6 navigates to the URL, locates the input element, and asserts if it is enabled or not. Since it is not enabled, the test case fails in the third line without moving forward.

Syntax

toBeEnabled()

Listing 4-6. toBeEnabled() Assertion

```
it('TC076_toBeEnabled()', () => {
    browser.url('https://the-internet.herokuapp.com/
    dynamic_controls')
    var elem = $('input[type="text"]')
    expect(elem).toBeEnabled()
    $('button=Enable').click() //won't get executed
    browser.pause(5000) //won't get executed
    var elem = $('input[type="text"]') //won't get executed
    expect(elem).toBeEnabled() //won't get executed
})
```

Output

```
Spec Files:      0 passed, 1 failed, 1 total (100% completed)
in 00:00:23
```

```
[chrome 87.0.4280.66 windows #0-0] Expect $(`input[type="text"]`) to be enabled
Expected: "enabled"
Received: "not enabled"
```

Figure 4-10. Console showing terminal output

Notes

The control didn't go past the first assertion in line 3. This is a bad practice because it leaves a dead code log in your automation. A good practice always puts the assertion at the end. Another way to write line 3 in Listing 4-6 uses expect(elem).not.toBeDisabled().

Is the Element Disabled?: toBeDisabled()

toBeDisabled() is an assertion that determines if the element is disabled or not. Listing 4-7 results in a passed test because the input field is disabled on the web page, as shown in Figure 4-11.

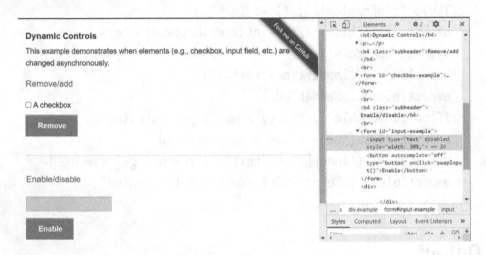

Figure 4-11. *A disabled input box, apparent from UI and seen in Chrome DevTools*

Syntax

toBeDisabled()

Listing 4-7. toBeDisabled() Assertion

```
it('TC077_toBeDisabled()', () => {
    browser.url('https://the-internet.herokuapp.com/
    dynamic_controls')
    var elem = $('input[type="text"]')
    expect(elem).toBeDisabled()
})
```

Output

```
Spec Files:      1 passed, 1 total (100% completed) in 00:00:15
```

Notes

Another way to write the assertion in Listing 4-7 is to use expect(elem).
not.toBeEnabled().

Is the Element Visible?: isDisplayed()

There are times when elements are present but hidden in a web page.
The isDisplayed() method identifies if an element is hidden or visible
and responds in the form of a Boolean true or false. Listing 4-8 shows the
isDisplayed() method in action. The user navigates to a URL and clicks
a Start button in Figure 4-12. Since the Start button is dynamic and takes
time to make the hidden element visible, if you verify it immediately after
clicking the Start button, you get a false response, as expected. After 7
seconds, you apply isDisplayed() and get the expected true response
because the element became visible in that time.

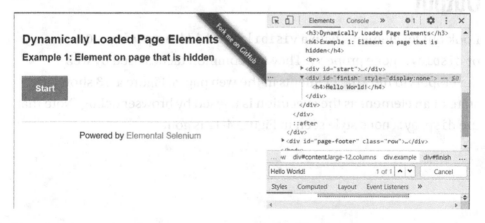

Figure 4-12.   *Start button present in the web page*

129

Syntax

isDisplayed()

Listing 4-8. isDisplayed() Element API

```
it('TC078_isDisplayed()', () => {
    browser.url('https://the-internet.herokuapp.com/
    dynamic_loading/1')
    $('button=Start').click()
    var elem = $('#finish')
    console.log('Visibility of element: Right after Start
    button clicked= ')
    console.log(elem.isDisplayed())
    browser.pause(7000)
    var elem = $('#finish')
    console.log('Verifying Visibility of element: After
    7 second pause= ')
    console.log(elem.isDisplayed())
})
```

Output

Look out for elements with a visibility: hidden, opacity: 0, or display: none property. They are common tactics used by web developers to hide the elements in the web pages. Figure 4-13 shows the state of an element as the execution is paused by browser.debug. Note that the display: none style seen in Figure 4-12 is gone.

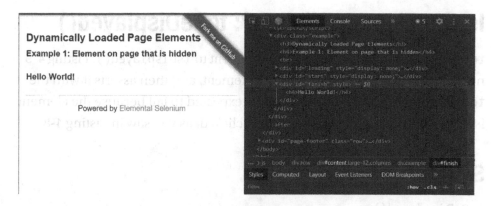

Figure 4-13. *State of <div> with id finish after Start button is clicked*

```
[0-0] Visibility of element: Right after Start button clicked=
[0-0] false
[0-0] Verifying Visibility of element: After 7 second pause=
[0-0] true
[0-0] Debugger listenin[0-0] g on ws://127.0.0.1:9229/60835a98-5315-4bf4-8b46-c77de2311f81
For help, see: https://nodejs.org/en/docs/inspector

The execution has stopped!
You can now go into the browser or use the command line as REPL
(To exit, press ^C again or type .exit)

[0-0] ›
(To exit, press ^C again or ^D or type .exit)
[0-0] ›
[0-0] PASSED in chrome - F:\Automation\WebdriverIO_0709\test\specs\basic.js
```

Figure 4-14. *The output in the console*

Notes

isDisplayed() is a Selenium WebDriver method introduced in Selenium 2.
It should not be confused with the old Selenium RC's isVisible()
method, which was depreciated.

Is the Element Visible?: toBeDisplayed()

toBeDisplayed() is an assertion equivalent to isDisplayed(). Listing 4-9 navigates to the URL and locates the element, and then asserts it with the toBeDisplayed() API. The test case is expected to fail because the element is not visible unless the Start button is clicked, as you saw in Listing 4-8.

Syntax

toBeDisplayed()

Listing 4-9. toBeDisplayed() Assertion

```
it('TC079_toBeDisplayed()', () => {
    browser.url('https://the-internet.herokuapp.com/
    dynamic_loading/2')
    var elem = $('#finish')
    expect(elem).toBeDisplayed()
})
```

Output

```
Spec Files:      0 passed, 1 failed, 1 total (100% completed)
in 00:00:21
```

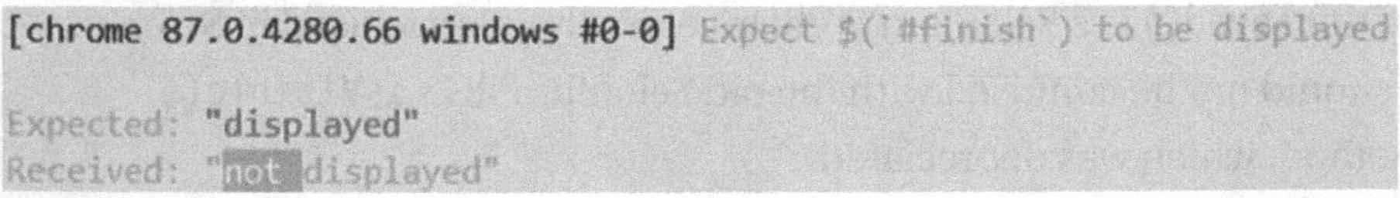

[chrome 87.0.4280.66 windows #0-0] Expect $('#finish') to be displayed

Expected: "displayed"
Received: "not displayed"

Figure 4-15. *The output in the console*

Notes

toBeDisplayed() calls the isDisplayed() function on a given element and asserts it.

Is the Element Visible?: toBeVisible()

toBeVisible() is the same as the toBeDisplayed() method for asserting whether an element is visible or not. They can be used interchangeably, depending on your validation lingo (see Listing 4-10).

Syntax

toBeVisible()

Listing 4-10. toBeVisible() Assertion

```
it('TCO80_toBeVisible()', () => {
    browser.url('https://the-internet.herokuapp.com/
    dynamic_loading/2')
    var elem = $('#finish')
    expect(elem).toBeVisible()
})
```

Output

This code is expected to fail, as shown in Figure 4-16.

```
Spec Files:      0 passed, 1 failed, 1 total (100% completed)
in 00:00:21
```

```
[chrome 87.0.4280.66 windows #0-0] Expect $('#finish') to be visible

Expected: "visible"
Received: "not visible"
```

Figure 4-16. *The output in the console*

Is the Element Visible on the screen?: toBeDisplayedInViewport()

The difference between toBeDisplayed() and toBeDiplayedInviewport() is that the latter method only verifies that the element is visible in the screen currently in view. If you need to scroll down to see the element, the test fails for that element. In Listing 4-11, the element is the first on the list and appears without browser maximization, so the test passes.

Syntax

toBeDisplayedInViewport()

Listing 4-11. toBeDisplayedInViewport() Assertion

```
it('TC081_toBeDisplayedInViewport()', () => {
    browser.url('https://the-internet.herokuapp.com/')
    var elem = $('=A/B Testing') //First Element from the list
    expect(elem).toBeDisplayedInViewport()
 })
```

Output

```
INFO webdriver: RESULT true
Spec Files:       1 passed, 1 total (100% completed) in 00:00:13
```

Notes

The function identifies whether the element is visible on your screen.
If the element is visible in the DOM but currently not on the screen, then it
is false.

Is the Element Visible on the Screen?: toBeVisibleInViewport()

The toBeVisibleInViewport() function is exactly like
toBeDisplayedInViewport(). In Listing 4-12, the function identifies
whether the element is visible on your screen. If the element is visible in
the DOM but currently not seen on the screen, then it fails, as in
Listing 4-13.

Syntax

toBeVisibleInViewport()

Listing 4-12. Using toBeVisibleInViewport() Assertion to Check If
the First Element Is Visible in Current Viewport

```
it('TC082_toBeVisibleInViewport()', () => {
    browser.url('https://the-internet.herokuapp.com/')
    var elem = $('=A/B Testing') //First Element from the list
    expect(elem).toBeVisibleInViewport()
})
```

Listing 4-13. Using toBeVisibleInViewport() Assertion to Check If the Last Element Is Visible in Current Viewport

```
it('TC083_toBeVisibleInViewport()', () => {
    browser.url('https://the-internet.herokuapp.com/')
    var elem = $('=WYSIWYG Editor') //Last Element from the
    list
    expect(elem).toBeVisibleInViewport()
})
```

Output

```
TC082-
INFO webdriver: RESULT true

TC083-
INFO webdriver: RESULT false
```

```
[chrome 87.0.4280.66 windows #0-0] Expect $(`=WYSIWYG Editor`) to be visible in viewport
Expected: "visible in viewport"
Received: "not visible in viewport"
```

Figure 4-17. *The output in the console*

Is the Element Selected?: isSelected()

The isSelected() method is usually applied to determine if the checkboxes are checked (selected) or not, as shown in Figure 4-18. This is not an assertion. Hence, it only returns true or false values to you; how you want to handle it beyond this is up to you. Two checkboxes are dealt with in Listing 4-14, where the first checkbox is unchecked and the second is checked. You locate and apply isSelected() method on both checkbox elements and get a true and a false output, respectively.

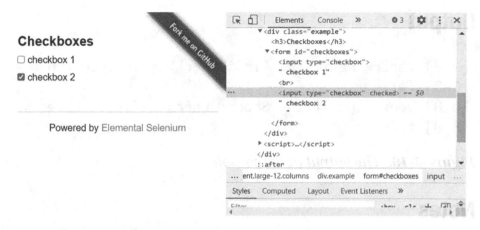

Figure 4-18. *Checkboxes present in the web page*

Syntax

isSelected()

Listing 4-14. isSelected() Element API

```
it('TC084_isSelected()', () => {
    browser.url('https://the-internet.herokuapp.com/
    checkboxes')
    var ChkBox1 = $$('input[type="checkbox"]')[0]
    console.log('Verifying if the First Checkbox is
    selected = ')
    console.log(ChkBox1.isSelected())
    var ChkBox2 = $$('input[type="checkbox"]')[1]
    console.log('Verifying if the Second Checkbox is
    selected = ')
    console.log(ChkBox2.isSelected())
})
```

Output

```
[0-0] Verifying if the First Checkbox is selected =
[0-0] false
[0-0] Verifying if the Second Checkbox is selected =
[0-0] true
```

Figure 4-19. *The output in the console*

Notes

Web developers use the `selected` property or the `checked` property; for example, `<input type="checkbox" checked="">`. Figure 4-18 shows the difference between an unchecked (checkbox 1) and a checked (checkbox 2) box.

Is the Element Selected?: toBeSelected()

toBeSelected() is the assertion equivalent of the isSelected() API. It passes or fails your test, as shown in Listings 4-15 and 4-16, respectively.

Syntax

```
toBeSelected()
```

Listing 4-15. toBeSelected() Assertion on First Checkbox

```
it('TC085_toBeSelected()', () => {
    browser.url('https://the-internet.herokuapp.com/
    checkboxes')
    var chkBox1 = $$('input[type="checkbox"]')[0]
    expect(chkBox1).toBeSelected()
})
```

Listing 4-16. toBeSelected() Assertion on Second Checkbox

```
it('TC086_toBeSelected()', () => {
    browser.url('https://the-internet.herokuapp.com/
    checkboxes')
    var chkBox2 = $$('input[type="checkbox"]')[1]
    expect(chkBox2).toBeSelected()
})
```

Output

TC085-

```
[chrome 87.0.4280.66 windows #0-0] Expect $('input[type="checkbox"]') to be selected
Expected: "selected"
Received: "not selected"
```

Figure 4-20. *The output in the console*

TC086-
INFO webdriver: RESULT true

Is the Element Selected?: toBeChecked()

The toBeChecked() method is the same as the toBeSelected() assertion method, as shown in Listings 4-17 and 4-18. The first test case fails, and the second test case passes.

Syntax

toBeChecked()

Listing 4-17. toBeChecked() Assertion on First Checkbox

```
it('TC087_toBeChecked()', () => {
    browser.url('https://the-internet.herokuapp.com/
    checkboxes')
    var chkBox1 = $$('input[type="checkbox"]')[0]
    expect(chkBox1).toBeChecked()
})
```

Listing 4-18. toBeChecked() Assertion on Second Checkbox

```
it('TC088_toBeChecked()', () => {
    browser.url('https://the-internet.herokuapp.com/
    checkboxes')
    var chkBox2 = $$('input[type="checkbox"]')[1]
    expect(chkBox2).toBeChecked()
})
```

Output

TC087-

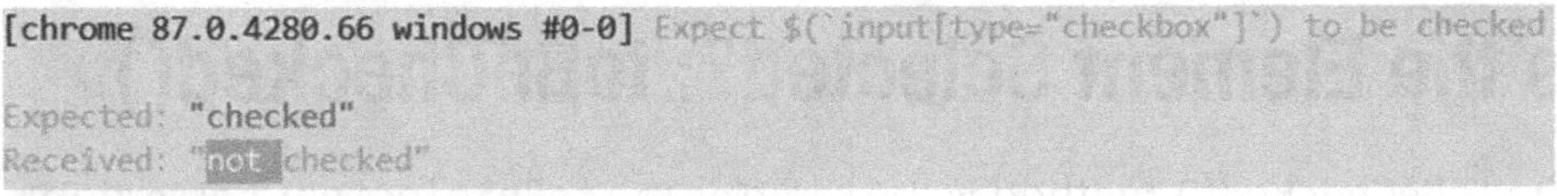

[chrome 87.0.4280.66 windows #0-0] Expect $(`input[type="checkbox"]`) to be checked

Expected: "checked"
Received: "not checked"

Figure 4-21. *The output in the console*

TC088-
INFO webdriver: RESULT true

Is the Element Clickable?: isClickable()

This method determines if the element is clickable and returns a Boolean result accordingly. Listing 4-19 navigates the URL and finds a button, as shown in Figure 4-22. It then applies the isClickable() method to see if it is clickable. The output returns false because the button is not clickable.

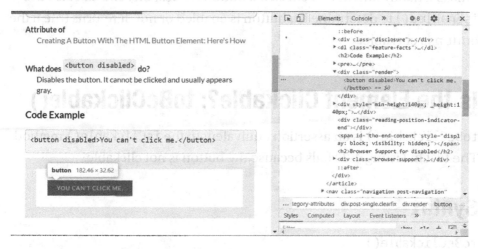

Figure 4-22. *Disabled button on a web site*

Syntax

isClickable()

Listing 4-19. isClickable() Element API on a Button

```
it('TC089_isClickable()', () => {
    browser.url('https://html.com/attributes/button-disabled/')
    var btn = $('button=You can\'t click me.')
    console.log(' Verifying if the button is clickable: ' +
    btn.isClickable())
})
```

Output

```
Verifying if the button is clickable= false
```

Notes

This is a handy function to check if a button is clickable. You can also use
`isEnabled()` to determine if a button is enabled or not. It returns true if the
button is clickable.

Is the Element Clickable?: toBeClickable()

`toBeClickable()` is an assertion equivalent to the `isClickable()` method.
The test in Listing 4-20 fails because the button is not clickable.

Syntax

```
toBeClickable()
```

Listing 4-20. toBeClickable() Assertion on a Button

```
it('TC090_isClickable()', () => {
    browser.url('https://html.com/attributes/button-disabled/')
    var btn = $('button=You can\'t click me.')
    expect(btn).toBeClickable()
})
```

Output

```
[chrome 87.0.4280.66 windows #0-0] Expect $( button=You can't click me.') to be clickable

Expected: "clickable"
Received: not clickable"
```

Figure 4-23. *The output in the console*

Notes

It checks if an element can be clicked by calling isClickable() on the element and making the assertion.

To Sum It Up

This chapter covered many API use cases, from a simple unit test that handles intermittent ad pop-ups to more complex scenarios. Figure 4-24 shows a web page that displays an ad in front of the web site landing page.

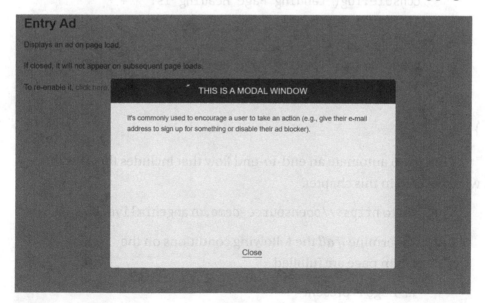

Figure 4-24. *Irregular ad pop-up on a web site*

An ad pop-up may be intermittent, so sometimes you see it, and sometimes you do not. You can handle this using an `if` condition combined with one of the APIs covered in this chapter, as shown in Listing 4-21. The code is looking for the `.modal-title` element. If found, the ad is present in the DOM. The code closes the ad, and prints the landing page title (i.e., Entry Ad). If the ad is not present, the code directly prints the landing page title. Apply `browser.debug` wherever you feel you need to monitor the page or an element's state.

Listing 4-21. Handling Intermittent Ads

```
it('TC_091 Handling Intermittent Ads', () => {
    browser.url('https://the-internet.herokuapp.com/entry_ad')
    var isAdPresent = $('.modal-title').isExisting()
    browser.pause(3000)
    if (isAdPresent == true) {
        $('p=Close').click()
        console.log('Landing Page Heading is: ' +
        $('<h3>').getText())
    } else {
        console.log('Landing Page Heading is: ' +
        $('<h3>').getText())
    }
})
```

Let's try to automate an end-to-end flow that includes the APIs that were covered in this chapter.

1. Go to `https://opensource-demo.orangehrmlive.com`.

2. Determine *if all* the following conditions on the Login page are fulfilled.

   a. Logo is present

   b. Username input field is enabled

    c. Password input field is enabled

    d. Submit button is visible and clickable

3. Go to the Login page and verify that the Quick Launch element is present in the landing page.

4. *Else* go to the Login with a warning and verify that the Quick Launch element is present in the landing page.

This is an end-to-end test. The final goal to verify that Quick Launch is loading on the landing page. You do not want your test case to fail in case of error in auxiliary validations, especially if you have hundreds of end-to-end cases to run in a preproduction environment with limited time. You could place warning mechanisms, as shown in Listing 4-22, during runtime so that your test cases don't fail unless they fail to achieve their main objective but still manage to throw appropriate warnings.

Listing 4-22. End-to-End Test Case with Primary Validation of Quick Launch Window in Dashboard of Landing Page and Auxiliary Validation of Login Page

```
it('TC_092 Login Journey', () => {
    browser.url('https://opensource-demo.orangehrmlive.com/')
    var isLogoPresent = $('#divLogo').isExisting()
    var isUsernameEnabled = $('#txtUsername').isEnabled()
    var isPasswordEnabled = $('#txtPassword').isEnabled()
    var isSubmitBtnDspld = $('#btnLogin').isDisplayed()
    var isSubmitBtnClkble = $('#btnLogin').isClickable()
    if (isLogoPresent && isUsernameEnabled && isPasswordEnabled
    && isSubmitBtnClkble && isSubmitBtnDspld) {
        $('#txtUsername').setValue('Admin')
        $('#txtPassword').setValue('admin123')
        $('#btnLogin').click()
```

```
        expect($('legend=Quick Launch')).toBePresent()
    } else {
        console.log('Issue Loading the Login Web page
        correctly')
        $('#txtUsername').setValue('Admin')
        $('#txtPassword').setValue('admin123')
        $('#btnLogin').click()
        expect($('legend=Quick Launch')).toBePresent()
    }
})
```

The code in Listing 4-22 will execute sucessfully; however, it is advisable you put the `browser.debug()` command whereever you require in the code to observe the state of the web page and its elements at any given point of time during the execution.

How to reduce duplication of code and abstract the recurring locators in our code is a discussion for later time. It will take place while we optimize the code in the framework and discuss design patters in the upcoming chapters.

Summary

The element APIs make your test cases more robust. You can use these APIs after successfully locating an element or right before interacting with the element. This ensures that the located element is in a dynamically interactable state during the runtime execution, before being acted upon by action commands and not in a hidden, disabled or unavailable state in the DOM.

The next chapter looks at additional WebdriverIO methods that are generally lesser used but can come in very handy in advanced test automation scenarios.

CHAPTER 5

Additional WebdriverIO Methods

So far, we have covered WebdriverIO installation, setup, locator strategies, and some widely used built-in methods to automate user actions. This chapter looks at additional WebdriverIO methods and built-in assertions that come in handy during end-to-end execution. Assertions are validation points that conclusively determine if a test case passed or failed. Assertions are hard validations, meaning the execution stops as soon as the control encounters an assertion statement.

Broadly, this chapter covers the following topics regarding elements.

- Focus

- Specific attributes

- Specific ID or class

- Specific property

- Specific text or value

- Specific link or href

- Count

© Shashank Shukla 2021
S. Shukla, *Practical WebDriverIO*, https://doi.org/10.1007/978-1-4842-6661-8_5

Is the Element Focused?: isFocused

isFocused() is an element API that returns *true* or *false*, depending on the element to determine if it has a focus on it. It is not an assertion, so the test carries on after returning the output. Listing 5-1 navigates to the URL and identifies the element to check the focus on; in this case, an input box, as shown in Figure 5-1. Next, the isFocused() method is applied. Since the input box was not clicked, the result is false (i.e., not focused). Next, the input box is clicked and the isFocused method is applied again. Since the input box was clicked and then isFocused was applied, the method returns true as shown in Figure 5-2.

Inputs

Number

Figure 5-1. *Input box on the web page*

Syntax

isFocused()

Listing 5-1. isFocused() Element API

```
it('TC091_isFocused()', () => {
    browser.url('https://the-internet.herokuapp.com/inputs')
    var inputBox = $('input[type="number"]')
    console.log("When input box is not clicked= ")
    console.log(inputBox.isFocused())
    inputBox.click()
```

```
    console.log("When input box is clicked= ")
    console.log(inputBox.isFocused())
})
```

Output

```
    [0-0] When input box is not clicked=
    [0-0] false
    [0-0] When input box is clicked=
    [0-0] true
```

Figure 5-2. *Console showing terminal output*

Note

If there are multiple elements present in DOM that are matched by the selector, then isFocused returns true for the element, which currently has focus on it.

Is the Element Focused?: toBeFocused

toBeFocused() is an assertion equivalent to the isFocused() method. It passes or fails a test script depending on the result of the toBeFocused() method. In this case, Listing 5-2 fails as shown in Figure 5-3 because the focus is not available on the input button since it hasn't been clicked. You also find in Listing 5-2 the expect() keyword, introduced in the last chapter. This keyword is derived from the @wdio/mocha-framework dependency included in the package.json file. It has a dependency on the expect-webdriverio npm package. WebdriverIO uses the expect() keyword to implement its built-in assertion functionality.

You can find more information is at the following.

- https://webdriver.io/docs/api/expect.html

- www.npmjs.com/package/expect-webdriverio

Syntax

toBeFocused()

Listing 5-2. toBeFocused() Assertion

```
it('TC092_toBeFocused()', () => {
    browser.url('https://the-internet.herokuapp.com/inputs')
    console.log("When input box is not clicked= ")
    var inputBox = $('input[type="number"]')
    expect(inputBox).toBeFocused()
})
```

Output

```
Spec Files:        0 passed, 1 failed, 1 total (100% completed)
in 00:00:21
```

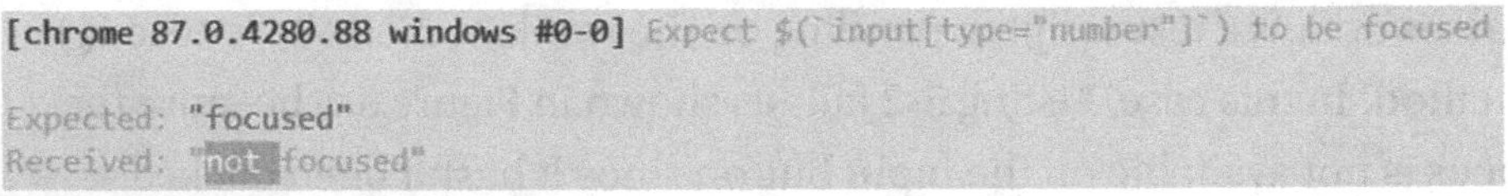

```
[chrome 87.0.4280.88 windows #0-0] Expect $('input[type="number"]') to be focused

Expected: "focused"
Received: "not focused"
```

Figure 5-3. *Console showing assertion failed in the terminal*

Note

It makes an assertion using the isFocused() function.

Does the Element Have a Specific Attribute?: toHaveAttribute

This assertion validates the expected value against an element's attribute. Figure 5-4 shows the <a> tag element here in the web page has an href attribute associated to it in the HTML code. Listing 5-3 navigates to URL and captures the <a> tag in the elem variable. The assertion is then applied to the variable to verify if the href attribute contains a https://the-internet.herokuapp.com/redirect value eventually passing the test case as shown in Figure 5-5.

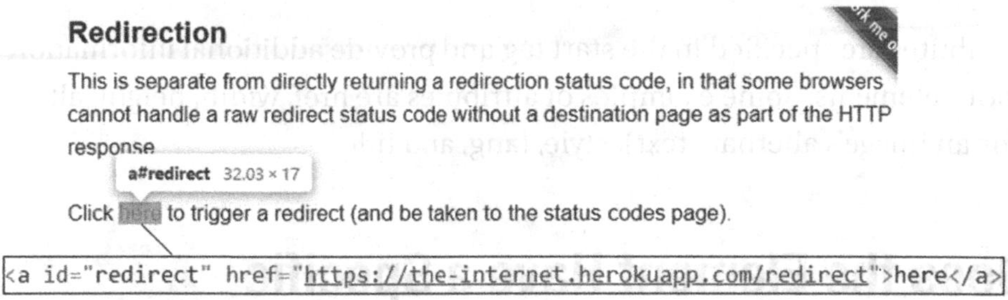

Redirection

This is separate from directly returning a redirection status code, in that some browsers cannot handle a raw redirect status code without a destination page as part of the HTTP response

a#redirect 32.03 × 17

Click here to trigger a redirect (and be taken to the status codes page).

`<a id="redirect" href="https://the-internet.herokuapp.com/redirect">here</a>`

Figure 5-4. Link here in <a> tag present on the web page

Syntax

toHaveAttribute()

Listing 5-3. API toHaveAttribute() Assertion

```
it('TC093_toHaveAttribute()', () => {
    browser.url('https://the-internet.herokuapp.com/
    redirector')
    var elem = $('#redirect')
    expect(elem).toHaveAttribute('href', 'https://the-internet.
    herokuapp.com/redirect')
})
```

Output

```
1 passing (4.7s)
Spec Files:       1 passed, 1 total (100% completed) in 00:00:10
```

```
242e95c4b2fad38a5ae6726180/element/3b000af6-bda5-441c-9f19-35762a2da2b4/attribute/h
ref
2020-12-11T08:41:48.832Z INFO webdriver: RESULT https://the-internet.herokuapp.com/
redirect
```

Figure 5-5. *Console showing output in the terminal*

Notes

Attributes are specified in the start tag and provide additional information about elements. Some examples of attributes are href, width, height, alt (for an image's alternate text), style, lang, and title.

Does the Element Have a Specific Attribute?: toHaveAttr

The toHaveAttr() assertion method's function is exactly like that of the toHaveAttribute() method. Let's look at it through a different example. Figure 5-6 shows three images present on the web page. The third image has a src attribute associated with the <img> tag. In Listing 5-4, we navigate to the URL of the web page and capture the third image's locator in a variable. Then we apply the toHaveAttr() method to this variable to validate if the src attribute's value matches our expected https://the internet.herokuapp.com/img/avatar-blank.jpg value. The test passes as shown in Figure 5-8 since the expected value as seen in Figure 5-7 matches the scr value in the HTML code shown in Figure 5-6.

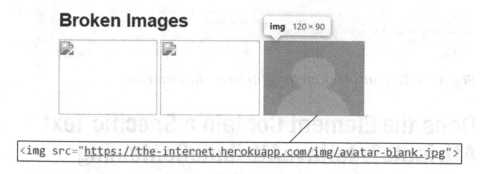

Figure 5-6. *Last image selected of the three Images available in DOM in <img> tag*

Syntax

toHaveAttr()

Listing 5-4. toHaveAttr() Assertion API

```
it('TC094_toHaveAttr()', () => {
    browser.url('https://the-internet.herokuapp.com/
    broken_images')
    var attr = $$('<img>')[3]
    expect(attr).toHaveAttr('src', 'https://the-internet.
    herokuapp.com/img/avatar-blank.jpg')
})
```

Output

```
1 passing (5.6s)
Spec Files:     1 passed, 1 total (100% completed) in 00:00:12
```

```
[0-0] 2020-12-10T08:28:10.944Z INFO webdriver: COMMAND getElementAttribute("a0ae634b-3a19-4648-833d-9f90356295
[0-0] 2020-12-10T08:28:10.944Z INFO webdriver: [GET] http://localhost:9515/session/bc06334c01de24c4ee5ec98862f
ae634b-3a19-4648-833d-9f903562957d/attribute/src
[0-0] 2020-12-10T08:28:10.957Z INFO webdriver: RESULT https://the-internet.herokuapp.com/img/avatar-blank.jpg
[0-0] 2020-12-10T08:28:10.961Z INFO webdriver: COMMAND deleteSession()
```

Figure 5-7. *Console showing output in the terminal*

Does the Element Contain a Specific Text Attribute?: toHaveAttributeContaining

The toHaveAttributeContaining() method is similar to
toHaveAttribute(), but it can partially match the string provided by
the user. To test the previous example with this method, in Listing 5-5, I
have only provided a .jpg string to see if there is a valid .jpg file present in
the src, regardless of the filename. The test passes as shown in Figure 5-8
because .jpg is part of the image URL in the <img> tag's src attribute.

Syntax

toHaveAttributeContaining()

Listing 5-5. toHaveAttributeContaining() Assertion API

```
it('TC095_ toHaveAttributeContaining()', () => {
    browser.url('https://the-internet.herokuapp.com/
    broken_images')
    var attr = $$('<img>')[3]
    expect(attr).toHaveAttributeContaining('src', '.jpg')
})
```

Output

```
1 passing (5.6s)
Spec Files:       1 passed, 1 total (100% completed) in 00:00:11
```

```
2020-12-10T08:32:11.837Z INFO webdriver: [GET] http://localhost:9515/session/dbbc24e421b90ba73ca97db5c7c
/e8729fd0-87f8-4c08-9ce4-4401f22025ed/attribute/src
2020-12-10T08:32:11.855Z INFO webdriver: RESULT https://the-internet.herokuapp.com/img/avatar-blank.jpg
2020-12-10T08:32:11.862Z INFO webdriver: COMMAND deleteSession()
```

Figure 5-8. *Console showing output in the terminal*

Notes

Be advised that the method is case sensitive; hence, .JPG (all caps) in
Listing 5-5 fails the test case.

Does the Element Have a Specific Class?: toHaveClass

The toHaveClass method matches the identified element's class with
user input. In Listing 5-6, the user navigates to the URL and identifies the
element whose class needs to be validated (in this case, an <h1> header
tag) and verifies if the header tag contains a header class name. Figure 5-9
shows the header class, and the test case in Figure 5-10 passes.

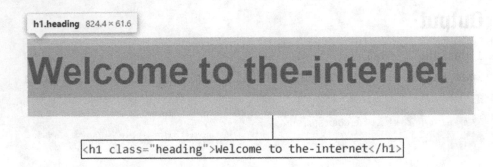

Figure 5-9. *Heading tag <h1> available on web page*

Syntax

```
toHaveClass()
```

Listing 5-6. toHaveClass() Assertion API

```
it('TC096_toHaveClass()', () => {
    browser.url('https://the-internet.herokuapp.com/')
    var HeadingTag = $('<h1>')
    expect(HeadingTag).toHaveClass('heading', {
        message: 'Not a "heading" class!',
    })
})
```

Output

```
1 passing (5s)
Spec Files:      1 passed, 1 total (100% completed) in 00:00:11
```

```
2020-12-10T08:34:23.616Z INFO webdriver: [GET] http://localhost:9515/se
/6ee775b8-dcf0-49d5-b1cb-b7dd1c69cb1a/attribute/class
[0-0] 2020-12-10T08:34:23.632Z INFO webdriver: RESULT heading
[0-0] 2020-12-10T08:34:23.638Z INFO webdriver: COMMAND deleteSession()
```

Figure 5-10. *Console showing output in the terminal*

Notes

If you give any selector an element that doesn't have the header class, the Not a "heading" class! customized error is thrown.

Does the Element Contain Specific Text in Class?: toHaveClassContaining

The toHaveClassContaining() method is similar to toHaveClass() with one difference. It can partially match the string provided by the user. Figure 5-11 shows a web page with a jQuery menu item. The <ul> menu tag contains many classes. Listing 5-7 validates any of the classes that match the of ui-menu value. The test passes in Figure 5-12 because the ui-menu class is one of the three classes, as you can see in Figure 5-11.

Syntax

toHaveClassContaining()

JQueryUI - Menu

JQuery UI Menus are a nice UI element from a user perspective, but
poses an interesting automation challenge since it requires mouse
operations and synchronization between them.

Another 'fun' aspect is that the visibility of elements is actually not in the
html itself, but done magically by JQuery so you cannot trust exactly what
the html is telling you. A user cannot fire click events at certain UI

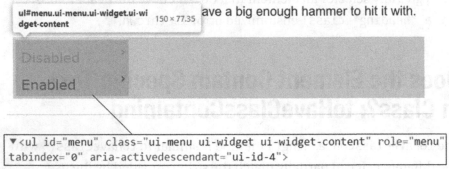

Figure 5-11. *jQuery menu item highlighted in Chrome DevTools*

Listing 5-7. toHaveClassContaining() Assertion API

```
it('TC097_toHaveClassContaining()', () => {
    browser.url('https://the-internet.herokuapp.com/jqueryui/
    menu')
    var menu = $('#menu')
    expect(menu).toHaveClassContaining('ui-menu')
})
```

Output

```
1 passing (8.9s)
Spec Files:      1 passed, 1 total (100% completed) in 00:00:19
```

```
[0-0] 2020-12-10T08:45:15.158Z INFO webdriver: [GET] http://localhost:9515/session/:
9b/element/194ae953-1162-40e1-82f7-36478a325cee/attribute/class
2020-12-10T08:45:15.168Z INFO webdriver: RESULT ui-menu ui-widget ui-widget-content
[0-0] 2020-12-10T08:45:15.176Z INFO webdriver: COMMAND deleteSession()
```

Figure 5-12. Console showing output in the terminal

Notes

The toHaveClassContaining() method is case sensitive.

Does the Element Have a Specific Property?: toHaveElementProperty

The toHaveElementProperty() method checks if an element has a certain property and matches it with user-provided input. In Figure 5-13 you can see three images. The third one (on the extreme right) has a height property of 90, as seen in the Chrome developer tools in Figure 5-13. Listing 5-8 navigates to the URL and locates the third image by using the TagName locator and holds it in elem variable. Then toHaveElementProperty() is applied on this variable to verify if the height is 90 pixels. As you already know, the height is 90 pixels, and the test case in Figure 5-14 passes with Result displayed as 90.

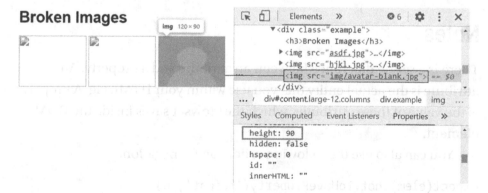

Figure 5-13. Height property of the image as displayed in Chrome developer tools on the browser

Syntax

```
toHaveElementProperty()
```

Listing 5-8. toHaveElementProperty() Assertion API

```
it('TC098_toHaveElementProperty()', () => {
    browser.url('https://the-internet.herokuapp.com/
    broken_images')
    var elem = $$('<img>')[3]
    expect(elem).toHaveElementProperty('height', 90)
})
```

Output

```
1 passing (4.4s)
Spec Files:      1 passed, 1 total (100% completed) in 00:00:11
```

```
[0-0] 2020-12-10T08:56:07.438Z INFO webdriver: [GET] http://localhost:9
0b/element/cce66037-077c-4c54-9e10-af8973d59d2f/property/height
[0-0] 2020-12-10T08:56:07.487Z INFO webdriver: RESULT 90
[0-0] 2020-12-10T08:56:07.492Z INFO webdriver: COMMAND deleteSession()
```

Figure 5-14. *Console showing output in the terminal*

Notes

There is a subtle difference between an attribute and a property. An attribute is the actual entity that you use within your HTML tag. A property is the value of these attributes, which the browser saves inside the DOM element.

You can also use the following validation for negation.

```
expect(elem).not.toHaveProperty('height', 0)
```

Does the Element Have a Specific Value?: toHaveValue

The toHaveValue() method checks if the element has a specific value and validates it against a user-provided value in the test. In Listing 5-9, the user navigates to a web site, locates the demo element, and validates if the element has a https://jqueryui.com/demos/ value as shown in Figure 5-15.

Syntax

toHaveValue()

Listing 5-9. toHaveValue() Assertion API

```
it('TCO99_toHaveValue()', () => {
    browser.url('https://jqueryui.com/')
    var elem = $('option[value="https://jqueryui.com/demos/"]')
    expect(elem).toHaveValue('https://jqueryui.com/demos/', {
        ignoreCase: true
    })
})
```

Output

```
1 passing (3.7s)
Spec Files:      1 passed, 1 total (100% completed) in 00:00:10
```

```
2b/element/5ad1f103-df8c-4ba3-ab6a-dfcf16710ab4/property/value
2020-12-10T08:57:34.030Z INFO webdriver: RESULT https://jqueryui.com/demos/
2020-12-10T08:57:34.035Z INFO webdriver: COMMAND deleteSession()
```

Figure 5-15. Console showing output in the terminal

Notes

The ignoreCase parameter matches the value regardless of its case.

Does the Element Have a Specific href?: toHaveHref

The toHaveHref() method checks if the <a> tag has a specific href value and validates it against the user-provided value in the test. In Listing 5-10, the user navigates to the web site and locates the demo element using the LinkText locator and validates if the element has an https://jqueryui.com/demos/ href attribute as seen in the console output in Figure 5-16.

Syntax

```
toHaveHref()
```

Listing 5-10. toHaveHref() Assertion API

```
it('TC100_toHaveHref()', () => {
    browser.url('https://jqueryui.com/')
    var elem = $('=demos')
    expect(elem).toHaveHref('https://jqueryui.com/demos/')
})
```

Output

```
1 passing (4.5s)
Spec Files:     1 passed, 1 total (100% completed) in 00:00:11
```

```
[0-0] 2020-12-10T08:59:13.07IZ INFO webdriver: [GET] http://localhost:9515/session
29/element/95f01b0b-96be-41d3-a76d-03edc87de663/attribute/href
[0-0] 2020-12-10T08:59:13.702Z INFO webdriver: RESULT https://jqueryui.com/demos/
[0-0] 2020-12-10T08:59:13.707Z INFO webdriver: COMMAND deleteSession()
```

Figure 5-16. *Console showing output in the terminal*

Notes

Checks if the link element has a specific link target.

Does the Element Contain a Specific Text in the href?: toHaveHrefContaining

The toHaveHrefContaining() method is similar to toHaveHref() with one difference; it can partially match the string provided by the user. Listing 5-11 validates if the string provided by the user matches any part of element's href. The test as its seen in Figure 5-17 passes because the /demos/ class is part of the URL in the HTML.

Syntax

```
toHaveHrefContaining()
```

Listing 5-11. toHaveHrefContaining() Assertion API

```
it('TC0101_toHaveHrefContaining()', () => {
    browser.url('https://jqueryui.com/')
    var elem = $('=demos')
    expect(elem).toHaveHrefContaining('/demos/')
})
```

Output

```
1 passing (14.5s)
Spec Files:       1 passed, 1 total (100% completed) in 00:00:21
```

```
e0/element/96c55333-2756-4e70-93ad-6401aea20920/attribute/href
2020-12-10T09:01:54.346Z INFO webdriver: RESULT https://jqueryui.com/demos/
[0-0] 2020-12-10T09:01:54.353Z INFO webdriver: COMMAND deleteSession()
```

Figure 5-17. *Console showing output in the terminal*

Does the Element Have a Specific Link?: toHaveLink

The toHaveLink method checks an <a> tag element to see if it contains a valid link. Listing 5-12 navigates to the web page and locates the About section in the nav bar. Once it is located, toHaveLink is applied to verify if it contains the https://jqueryui.com/about/ link which passes the test case as shown in Figure 5-18.

Syntax

```
toHaveLink()
```

Listing 5-12. toHaveLink() Assertion API

```
it('TC102_toHaveLink()', () => {
    browser.url('https://jqueryui.com/')
    const link = $('=About')
    expect(link).toHaveLink('https://jqueryui.com/about/')
})
```

Output

```
1 passing (8.1s)
Spec Files:        1 passed, 1 total (100% completed) in 00:00:15
```

```
[0-0] 2020-12-10T09:03:05.518Z INFO webdriver: [GET] http://localhost:9515/session
09/element/cd0f28f6-b39e-415a-b38e-766238e66446/attribute/href
[0-0] 2020-12-10T09:03:05.541Z INFO webdriver: RESULT https://jqueryui.com/about/
[0-0] 2020-12-10T09:03:05.548Z INFO webdriver: COMMAND deleteSession()
```

Figure 5-18. *Console showing output in the terminal*

Notes

It is the same as toHaveHref().

Does the Element Contain a Specific Text in the Link?: toHaveLinkContaining

toHaveLinkContaining() does the same thing as toHavelink() but it matches a partial link in the script against the link available in the element on the web page, as shown in Listing 5-13 and its output in Figure 5-19.

Syntax

```
toHaveLinkContaining()
```

Listing 5-13. toHaveLinkContaining() Assertion API

```
it('TC103_toHaveLinkContaining', () => {
    browser.url('https://jqueryui.com/')
    const link = $('=About')
    expect(link).toHaveLinkContaining('/about/')
})
```

Output

```
1 passing (9.7s)
Spec Files:       1 passed, 1 total (100% completed) in 00:00:16
```

```
be/element/7ed6144b-818f-423c-8ec7-f21d96ff6a74/attribute/href
2020-12-10T09:19:46.119Z INFO webdriver: RESULT https://jqueryui.com/about/
[0-0] 2020-12-10T09:19:46.126Z INFO webdriver: COMMAND deleteSession()
```

Figure 5-19. *Console showing output in the terminal*

Notes

It has the same notes as toHaveLinkContaining().

Does the Element Have a Specific Text?: toHaveText

The toHaveText method validates whether an element has an associated text and returns true if it matches the user's string in the test case, as shown in Listing 5-14. Since the h1 tag matched the string provided by the user, the test case passes with the Result as seen in Figure 5-20.

Syntax

```
toHaveText()
```

Listing 5-14. toHaveText() Assertion API

```
it('TC104_toHaveText', () => {
    browser.url('https://the-internet.herokuapp.com/')
    const text = $('<h1>')
    expect(text).toHaveText('Welcome to the-internet')
})
```

Output

```
1 passing (14.3s)
Spec Files:       1 passed, 1 total (100% completed) in 00:00:20
```

```
[0-0] 2020-12-10T09:31:42.343Z INFO webdriver: [GET] http://localhost:9515/se
06/element/a9fc0f53-f31d-4269-a41b-626c41a269c1/text
[0-0] 2020-12-10T09:31:42.391Z INFO webdriver: RESULT Welcome to the-internet
[0-0] 2020-12-10T09:31:42.398Z INFO webdriver: COMMAND deleteSession()
```

Figure 5-20. *Console showing output in the terminal*

Notes

In Listing 5-14, I used the TagName selector since there is only one h1
available on the web page. However, this is not a foolproof way to identify a
unique element. If future developers add another h1 tag before the current
h1 tag, it will break the test because our code only identifies the first h1 it
encounters. In real-life scenarios, you must be a lot more sensitive about
the uniqueness and validity of the element being fetched by your selector
strategy.

Also, be advised that this matcher is case sensitive.

Does the Element Contain a Specific Text?: toHaveTextContaining()

The toHaveTextContaining() method validates if a string provided by
the user in the test case in Listing 5-15 is a substring of the text associated
with the elements on the web page and passes the test case as shown if
Figure 5-21.

Syntax

```
toHaveTextContaining()
```

Listing 5-15. toHaveTextContaining() Assertion API

```
it('TC105_toHaveTextContaining', () => {
    browser.url('https://the-internet.herokuapp.com/')
    const text = $('<h1 />')
    expect(text).toHaveTextContaining('internet')
})
```

Output

```
1 passing (9.4s)
Spec Files:       1 passed, 1 total (100% completed) in 00:00:15
```

```
[0-0] 2020-12-10T10:18:40.203Z INFO webdriver: [GET] http://localhost:9515/ses
f0/element/14e98328-bdb4-4783-b1ad-b83c117d68a5/text
[0-0] 2020-12-10T10:18:40.218Z INFO webdriver: RESULT Welcome to the-internet
[0-0] 2020-12-10T10:18:40.221Z INFO webdriver: COMMAND deleteSession()
```

Figure 5-21. Console showing output in the terminal

Does the Element Have a Specific ID?

The toHaveId() method validates whether an element on a web page has a specific ID locator, which the user provides in the test case in Listing 5-16 to get the output as a passed test case as shown in Figure 5-22.

Syntax

```
toHaveId()
```

Listing 5-16. toHaveId() Assertion API

```
it('TC106_toHaveId', () => {
    browser.url('https://the-internet.herokuapp.com/')
    const text = $$('.large-12.columns')[1]
    expect(text).toHaveId('content')
})
```

Output

```
1 passing (12s)
Spec Files:      1 passed, 1 total (100% completed) in 00:00:18
```

```
[0-0] 2020-12-11T04:36:08.658Z INFO webdriver: [GET] http://localhost:9
bute/id
[0-0] 2020-12-11T04:36:08.675Z INFO webdriver: RESULT content
[0-0] 2020-12-11T04:36:08.683Z INFO webdriver: COMMAND deleteSession()
```

Figure 5-22. *Console showing output in the terminal*

Element Count

The toBeElementsArrayOfSize() method provides an assertion to validate the length of an element's array fetched from $$(") or in the `FindElements` locator. In Listing 5-17, `$$('<input>')` fetches multiple elements since there are multiple fields present on the web page. It can be validated to ensure the actual result is exactly what the user expects. In this case, it is expected to fail as seen in Figure 5-23 because the number of input fields are not greater than or equal to (gte >=) 10.

Syntax

```
toBeElementsArrayOfSize()
```

Listing 5-17. toBeElementsArrayOfSize() Assertion API

```
it('TC107_Count of Element Returned', () => {
    browser.url('https://the-internet.herokuapp.com/
    checkboxes')
    console.log("")
    const elems = $$('<input>')
    expect(elems).toBeElementsArrayOfSize({
        gte: 10
        })
    })
```

Output

```
Spec Files:        0 passed, 1 failed, 1 total (100% completed)
in 00:00:27
```

```
[chrome 87.0.4280.88 windows #0-0] Expect $$(`<input>`) to be elements array of size

Expected: ">= 10"
Received: 2
```

Figure 5-23. *Console showing output in the terminal*

Notes

It is almost similar to `array.length`. `expect().toHaveChildren()` also serves the same purpose. `assert.ok(elems.length >= 10)` does the same task. You look at that assert method from the Chai library in upcoming chapters.

To Sum It Up

Let's look at some real-world, end-to-end examples of the APIs covered in this chapter using `https://opensource-demo.orangehrmlive.com`. First, read the following test case description and try it on your own. There is no specific output since the scripts end with `expect` assertions, making the test case either pass or fail. I did not make the script robust (to avoid adding complexity), so if the script fails, try to debug and understand the issue, and then fix it. I strongly recommend that you apply `browser. debug()` wherever necessary to better understand the execution flow.

Description: To validate the alternate text of the logo on the landing page as seen in Figure 5-24 after logging in is equal to string "OrangeHRM"

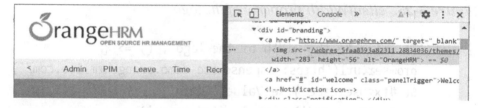

Figure 5-24. *Alternate text of logo*

```
it('To validate the alternate text of the logo is
"OrangeHRM"', () => {
    browser.url('https://opensource-demo.orangehrmlive.com/')
    $('#txtUsername').setValue('Admin')
    $('#txtPassword').setValue('admin123')
    $('#btnLogin').click()
    var logo = $('img[src*="logo"]')
    expect(logo).toHaveAttribute('alt', 'OrangeHRM')
})
```

1. First, validate the width of the OrangeHRM logo on the landing page after login (see Figure 5-25).

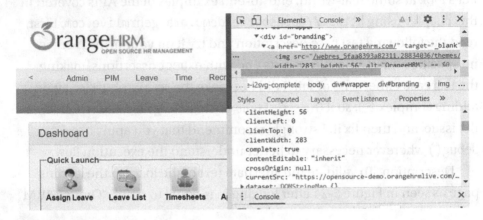

Figure 5-25. *clientWidth property of the logo*

```
it('To validate the width of the logo', () => {
    browser.url('https://opensource-demo.orangehrmlive.com/')
    $('#txtUsername').setValue('Admin')
    $('#txtPassword').setValue('admin123')
    $('#btnLogin').click()
    var logo = $('img[src*="logo"]')
    expect(logo).toHaveElementProperty('width', '283')
})
```

2. Next, validate that the user can navigate the Assign Leave form using keyboard controls (see Figure 5-26).

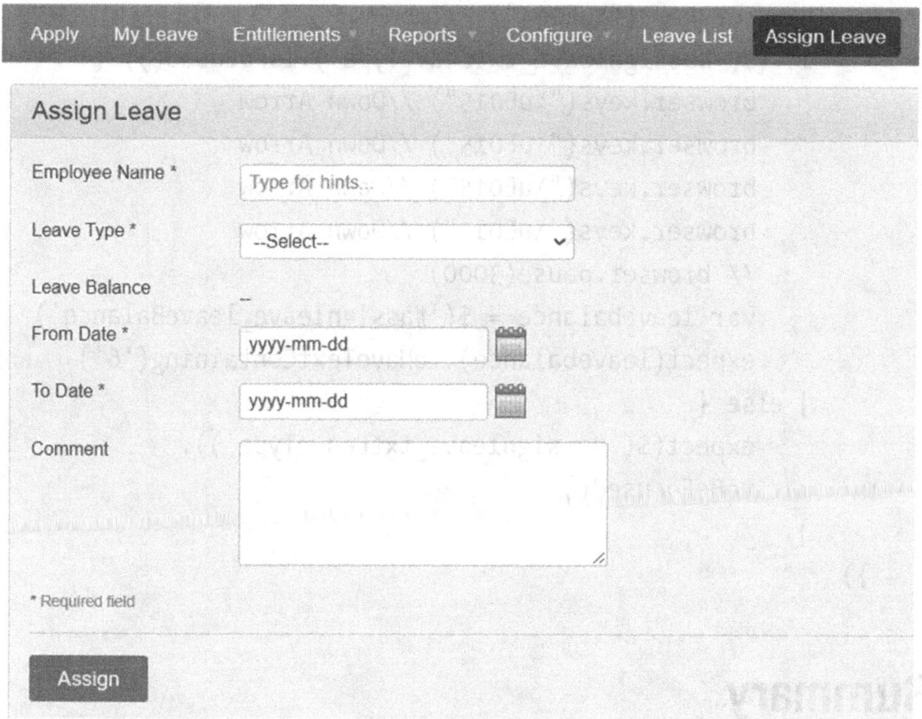

Figure 5-26. *Assign Leave form*

```
it('To validate the user is able to navigate 'Assign
Leaves' form using keyboard controls', () => {
    browser.url('https://opensource-demo.orangehrmlive.com/')
    $('#txtUsername').setValue('Admin')
    $('#txtPassword').setValue('admin123')
    $('#btnLogin').click()
    $('b=Leave').moveTo()
    $('a=Assign Leave').moveTo()
    $('a=Assign Leave').click()
    $('#assignleave_txtEmployee_empName').
    setValue("Jordan")
    browser.keys("\uE007") //Enter
```

```
        browser.keys("\uE004") //Tab
    if ($('#assignleave_txtLeaveType').isFocused()) {
        browser.keys("\uE015") //Down Arrow
        browser.keys("\uE015") //Down Arrow
        browser.keys("\uE015") //Down Arrow
        browser.keys("\uE015") //Down Arrow
        // browser.pause(3000)
        var leavebalance = $('#assignleave_leaveBalance')
        expect(leavebalance).toHaveTextContaining('6')
    } else {
        expect($('#assignleave_txtLeaveType')).
        toBeFocused()
    }
})
```

Summary

This chapter looked at a few more APIs and assertions that assist you in our automation journey, making your test cases robust and cleaner. In the next chapter, let's look at other APIs used in day-to-day automation tasks and that are good to know and have in your arsenal.

CHAPTER 6

Other Useful APIs

In this chapter, you learn more WebdriverIO API methods. These are methods that are good to know because they are often asked during interviews to check your knowledge. The chapter discusses the following.

- Shadow DOMS

- Getting an HTML page source and an element's HTML code

- Getting the active element, location, and size

- Getting the tag name, property, and CSS property

Dealing with a Shadow DOM

A shadow DOM encapsulates an element's DOM tree so that it can't accidentally be changed by the main document. For instance, suppose there is a web site that has a CSS class named errorText that has a color property defined as *red*, and you used an external library with a class named errorText that has a color property defined as *purple*, the result not always be what you expect (see Figure 6-1). The purple color property is applied to the My Text string instead of the red color property. You can check out the code at JSFiddle (`https://jsfiddle.net/h52jf438/`).

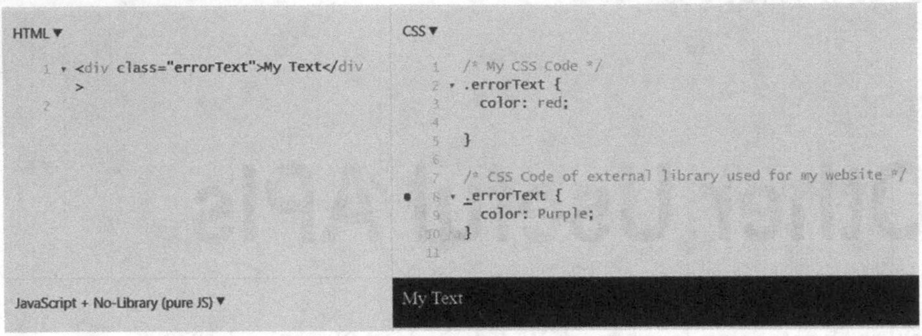

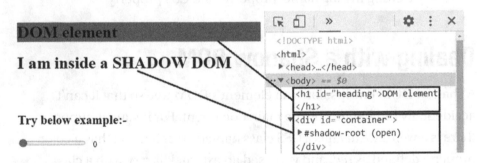

Figure 6-1. *HTML CSS and output of the code in JSFiddle*

In front-end design, when an external library is being called and used, there are other methods to solve this issue. A shadow DOM provides a local scoping that creates a fence between the web site code and external libraries used to develop the web site. To demonstrate a shadow DOM, Figure 6-2 shows two elements present in a small web page at `https://run.plnkr.co/plunks/RpYnoSbkkHidZO8d/`.

Figure 6-2. *Difference between regular DOM and shadow DOM elements*

Element h1 is available in the DOM, and the element inside div is not part of this DOM. If you want to verify this, click the drop-down you see in Figure 6.2. It expands to show you its contents, as shown in Figure 6-3.

```
▼<div id="container">
  ▼#shadow-root (open)
      <h1 id="inside">I am inside a SHADOW DOM
      </h1> == $0
  </div>
```

Figure 6-3. *Shadow DOM element reveals its HTML code*

Try to fetch it using the `findElement($('selector'))` API and its
"inside" ID; that is, `console.log($('#inside').getText());`.

You get the following error:

```
Can't call getText on element with selector "#inside" because
element wasn't found
```

The correct way is shown in Listing 6-1 using WebdriverIO's shadow
DOM command.

Syntax

`$(selector).shadow$$(selector)`

Listing 6-1. Finding the Shadow DOM Element and Fetching
Its Text

```
it('TC108_Shadow DOM', () => {
    browser.url('https://run.plnkr.co/plunks/
    RpYnoSbkkHidZO8d/')
    $('button=Proceed').click() //Plucker Phishing Warning
    console.log($('#heading').getText())
    console.log($('#container').shadow$('#inside').getText())
})
```

Output

```
DOM element
I am inside a SHADOW DOM
```

In most web sites, you cannot see the shadow DOM in the web site's DOM. Open Chrome DevTools by Ctrl+Shift+I. Follow the steps to enable shadow DOM visibility, as shown in Figure 6-4 and Figure 6-5.

1. In Chrome DevTools, open Settings (the three dots).

2. Click More Tools.

3. Click Settings.

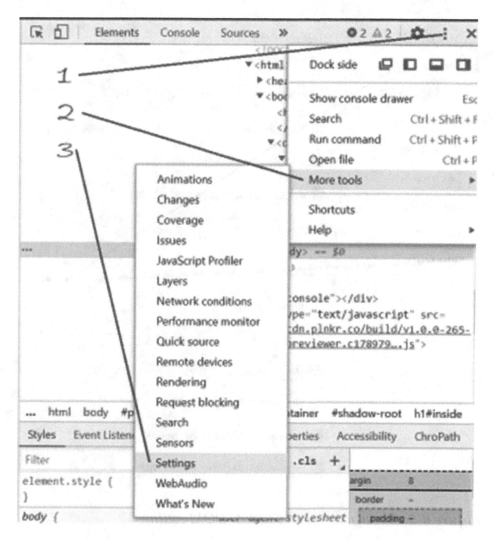

Figure 6-4. *Opening Chrome DevTools and navigating to Settings*

4.   Go to the Preference tab.

179

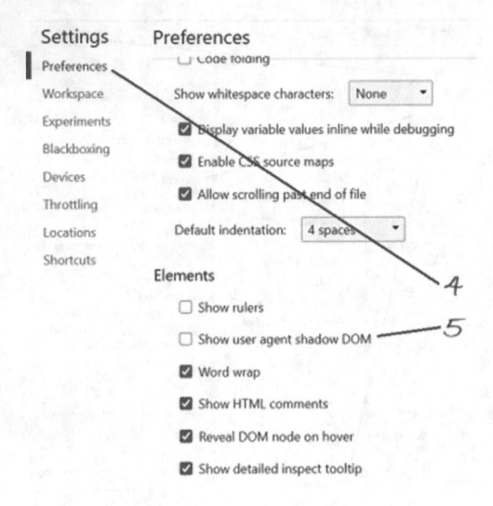

Figure 6-5. _Show user agent shadow DOM setting_

5. Make sure the "Show user agent shadow DOM"
   option is checked.

Getting the Page Source

To get the web page's HTML source, you can use the `browser.getPageSource()` command after navigating to the target web page, as shown in Listing 6-2.

Syntax

```
browser.getPageSource()
```

Listing 6-2. Fetching the Page Source of the Navigated URL

```
it('TC109_getPageSource', () => {
    browser.url('https://the-internet.herokuapp.com/')
    console.log(browser.getPageSource())
})
```

Output

```
[HTML Source Code of the URL]
```

It fetches the entire web page's source code. JavaScript-heavy sites might not show the same elements in the inspect element and view source. For these sites, Selenium needs to wait for jQuery/JS to load.

Getting an Active Element

`browser.getActiveElement()` returns the active element in the DOM currently in focus. In Listing 6-3, after navigating to the URL, you locate the input field and add value to it. Since it is the latest locator used, it is in focus. Hence, when you apply the `getActive` element and get its tag name, the same input field is returned.

Syntax

```
browser.getActiveElement()
```

Listing 6-3. Finding Active Element in the DOM

```
it('TC110_getActiveElement', () => {
    browser.url('https://www.saucedemo.com/')
    $('#user-name').addValue("standard_user")
    var elem = browser.getActiveElement()
    console.log("Tag name of active element is: " +
    $(elem).getTagName())
  })
```

Output

```
Tag name of active element is: input
```

Getting the Property of an Element

The $(selector).getProperty(property) command returns the element's property from the web page. Listing 6-4 shows the draggable property fetched for the located element via the #username selector. This demonstrates the difference between getProperty and getAttribute.

Syntax

```
$(selector).getProperty(property)
```

Listing 6-4. Getting Attribute and Property of the DOM Element

```
it('TC111_getProperty & getAttribute', () => {
    browser.url('https://the-internet.herokuapp.com/login')
    console.log("Property is: " + $('#username').
    getProperty('draggable'))
    console.log("Attribute is: " + $('#username').
    getAttribute('type'))

})
```

Output

```
Property is: false
Attribute is: text
```

Be advised that getProperty() and getAttribute() are different commands. In Figure 6-6, attributes are written while writing HTML code. Attributes are associated with a specific element. However, when the browser parses the HTML code, a corresponding DOM node is created. This node is an object, and therefore, it has properties associated with it, which are seen in the Chrome DevTools console in Figure 6-7.

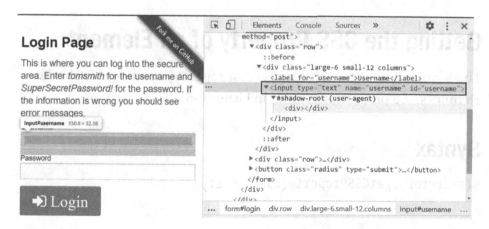

Figure 6-6. *Input tag with attributes type, name, and ID*

The attribute type, name, and ID are seen in Figure 6-6 for elements highlighted in the Elements section of DevTools.

In the Console section, the properties can be seen by using the `console.dir($0)` command, as depicted in Figure 6-7.

Figure 6-7.   *Properties associated with input tag*

Getting the CSS Property of an Element

The `$(selector).getCSSProperty(cssProperty)` command fetches the element's CSS property, as shown in Listing 6-5.

Syntax

`$(selector).getCSSProperty(cssProperty)`

Listing 6-5. Getting DOM Element CSS Property

```
it('TC112_getCSSProperty', () => {
    browser.url('https://the-internet.herokuapp.com/login')
    console.log("Font Family is- ", $('#username').
    getCSSProperty('font-family'))
})
```

Output

```
[0-0] Font Family is-  {
  property: 'font-family',
  value: 'helvetica neue',
  parsed: {
    value: [
      'helvetica neue',
      'helvetica',
      'helvetica',
      'arial',
      'sans-serif'
    ],
    type: 'font',
    string: '"helvetica neue", helvetica, helvetica, arial,
    sans-serif'
  }
}
```

This function extracts the CSS styles associated with an element. Some of the common CSS style properties are color, background-color, width, height, margin, border, font, and position.

Make sure that you don't use a + to concatenate any string with the result, which is an object returned by promise; use a , instead. Otherwise, the result be 'Font Family: [object Object]'.

Getting the Tag Name of an Element

The $(selector).getTagName() command gets an element's tag name, as shown in Listing 6-6. Commonly used tags are <a>, <div>, <ui>, <li>, <h1>, <h2>, <img>, and so forth.

Syntax

$(selector).getTagName()

Listing 6-6. Getting DOM Element TagName

```
it('TC113_getTagName', () => {
    browser.url('https://www.saucedemo.com/')
    console.log("Tagname is: " + $('.login_logo').getTagName())
})
```

Output

Tagname is: div

Getting the Location of an Element

The $(selector).getLocation(prop) method gets an element's location, as shown in Listing 6-7. Determining an element's location is useful in UI testing because it helps the user to match the object's position in terms of expected numbers without having to visually verify it. For example, you can verify the location of a logo, header, footer, and other elements by mentioning certain parameters and tolerance in your system tests.

Syntax

```
$(selector).getLocation(prop)
```

Listing 6-7. Getting Location of the DOM Element in Web Browser

```
it('TC114_getLocation function', () => {
    browser.url('https://the-internet.herokuapp.com/')
    const logo = $('<img>')
    const location = logo.getLocation()
    console.log("Location is: " + location)
    const xLocation = logo.getLocation('x')
    console.log("X Coordinate: " + xLocation)
    const yLocation = logo.getLocation('y')
    console.log("Y Coordinate: " + yLocation)
})
```

Output

```
Location is: { x: 763, y: 0 }
X Coordinate: 763
Y Coordinate: 0
```

These are not the exact location of an element on the web page; it depends on your desktop and browser size. Listing 6-8 shows the location of the same element when the browser isn't maximized vs. when the browser is maximized.

Listing 6-8. Element Location Is Not Absolute but Browser-Dependent

```
it('TC115_getLocation function', () => {
    browser.url('https://the-internet.herokuapp.com/')
    var logo1 = $('<img>')
    var location1 = logo1.getLocation()
    console.log(location1) // outputs: { x: 763, y: 0 }
    browser.maximizeWindow()
    var logo2 = $('<img>')
    var location2 = logo2.getLocation()
    console.log(location2) // outputs: { x: 1754, y: 0 }
})
```

Getting the Size of an Element

The $(selector).getSize(prop) method gets an element's size, as shown in Listing 6-9. The WebdriverIO getSize API schedules a command to compute the size (in pixels) of the element's bounding box. It can be used extensively when testing responsive web sites to ensure that the div and logos on the web site maintain a specific size when browser size differs.

Syntax

```
$(selector).getSize(prop)
```

Listing 6-9. Getting the DOM Element Size on Web Browser

```
it('TC116_getSize', () => {
    browser.url('https://the-internet.herokuapp.com/')
    const logo = $('<img>')
    const size = logo.getSize()
```

```
console.log("Size is: " + size)
const width = logo.getSize('width')
console.log("Width is " + width)
const height = logo.getSize('height')
console.log("Height is " + height)
})
```

Output

Size is: { width: 149, height: 149 }
Width is 149
Height is 149

Getting the HTML Build of an Element

The $(selector).getHTML({ }) method fetches the element's HTML code from its DOM, as shown in Listing 6-10.

Syntax

$(selector).getHTML({ })

Listing 6-10. Getting HTML Code of the DOM Element on Web Browser

```
it('TC117_Get HTML', () => {
    browser.url('https://www.saucedemo.com/')
    console.log("HTML is: " + $('#login-button').getHTML())
})
```

Output

```
HTML is: <input type="submit" class="btn_action" id="login-
button" value="LOGIN">
```

Summary

Although some of these API methods are not often used, it's always good to know about them. The next chapter looks at waits, which make our test cases more robust and run faster.

CHAPTER 7

Waits

This chapter discusses waits. Most flakiness in tests are due to race conditions between the browser and the user's instructions. When the browser lags, user instructions are executed even when the element is not available in the DOM. Eventually, the element loads afterward, depending on the network bandwidth's server response time or how animation-extensive the web page is.

There are two ways to handle the issue of WebdriverIO (or Selenium) needing to wait for an element: hard waits and explicit waits.

Hard and Explicit Waits at a Glance

Using hard-coded waits (static waits) before every statement (like we have done so far using the browser.pause command) is bad practice because it slows down the whole suite's execution. This is particularly noticeable if your test suite has thousands of tests to run.

Rather than using hard waits, a smarter approach uses dynamic *implicit* waits and *explicit* waits because they are reliable and faster. They always wait until the object/state is resolved and rely on actual object availability. They are generally faster when implemented correctly.

© Shashank Shukla 2021
S. Shukla, *Practical WebDriverIO*, https://doi.org/10.1007/978-1-4842-6661-8_7

Hard Sleep

Listing 7-1 shows that after clicking the Submit button, you wait for 10 seconds before the "Hello World" text appears. However, although the text appears a lot sooner than 10 seconds, the script waits for 10 seconds anyway, wasting time that could have been put into executing. And, this doesn't address scenarios where an application is slow, or there is an issue with the user's Internet speed.

The only decent use of a hard wait is that it allows you to observe a test case flow while developing it; however, the debug command you saw in the last chapter is still a better solution. In this chapter, you try to remove wait statements to observe the errors you encounter.

Syntax

```
browser.pause(milliseconds)
```

Listing 7-1. Hard Sleep of 10 Seconds Applied in the Test Script

```
it('TC119_Pause', () => {
    browser.url('https://the-internet.herokuapp.com/
    dynamic_loading/1')
    $('button=Start').click()
    browser.pause(10000)
    console.log('TEXT IS ' + $('#finish').$('<h4 />').
    getText())
})
```

Output

```
TEXT IS Hello World!
1 passing (14.5s)
Spec Files:       1 passed, 1 total (100% completed) in 00:00:21
```

Since this is a hard wait, WebdriverIO pauses and waits for 10 seconds no matter what before resuming the execution.

Wait for an Element to Be Clickable

Listing 7-2 demos an explicit wait, where the Click me!!! button is enabled in the DOM only after 3 seconds (see Figure 7-1). The code fetches the button by its ID, waits for it to be clickable, and as soon as it is clicked, it fetches the text displayed in the <p> tag.

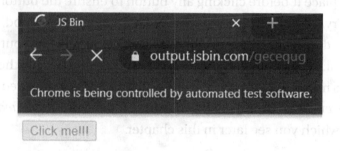

Figure 7-1. *Disabled Click me!!! button at the initial load*

Syntax

```
waitForClickable()
```

Listing 7-2. Waiting for Remove Button to Be Clickable

```
it('TC120_waitForClickable', () => {
    browser.url('https://output.jsbin.com/gecequg')
    var button = $('#MY_ID')
    button.waitForClickable()
```

```
    button.click()
    console.log("Text After Button click: " + $('#demo').
    getText())
})
```

Output

```
Text After Button click: YOU CLICKED ME!
```

waitForClickable() waits for the element to be clickable. It is good practice to place it before clicking any button to ensure the button is not disabled. Try the code without the waitforClickable() method, and observe the difference in the result. You can also place a {timeout: 5000} and {interval: 500} parameter within waitForClickable to tell the method to wait for a maximum of 5000 ms, or 5 seconds, before the timeout and retry every half second during this time. It's called a *fluent wait* in Selenium, which you see later in this chapter.

Wait for an Element to Be Displayed

Listing 7-3 features an explicit wait, where the element is waiting to become visible. The maximum timeout to wait is 10000 ms, or 10 seconds. Once the Start button is pressed, as shown in Figure 7-2, the element is visible in a few seconds. It is fetched via getText and displays in the terminal through console.log.

Dynamically Loaded Page Elements

Example 1: Element on page that is hidden

Figure 7-2. *Start button displays Hello World!*

Syntax

waitForDisplayed()

Listing 7-3. Waiting for Hello World! to Be Visible After Clicking Start Button

```
it('TC121_WaitForDisplayed', () => {
    browser.url('https://the-internet.herokuapp.com/
    dynamic_loading/1')
    $('button=Start').click()
    var elem = $('#finish')
    elem.waitForDisplayed({
        timeout: 10000
    })
    console.log('TEXT IS ' + $('#finish').$('<h4 />').
    getText())
})
```

195

Output

```
TEXT IS Hello World!
$(selector).waitForDisplayed({ timeout, reverse, timeoutMsg,
interval })
```

waitForDisplayed() also detects when the element is no longer visible in the DOM (but still present). In Listing 7-4, a 'reverse: true' parameter waits for the mydiv element to become invisible after 3 seconds, taking a screenshot before and after the event. A comparison of the screenshots is shown in Figure 7-3.

Listing 7-4. waitForDisplayed() Method With Reverse Parameter Set to True

```
it('TC122.1_Should detect when element is no longer visible',
() => {
    browser.url('https://output.jsbin.com/zivalup')
    browser.saveScreenshot('Screenshots/Before.png')
    const elem = $('#mydiv')
    elem.waitForDisplayed({
        reverse: true
    })
    browser.saveScreenshot('Screenshots/After.png')
})
```

Figure 7-3. Differences between before and after screenshots for waitForDisplayed method

Wait for an Element to Be Enabled

The waitForEnabled() command ensures that the WebdriverIO waits until the element is enabled in the DOM before any other action command is applied to it, as shown in Listing 7-5.

Syntax

```
waitForEnabled()
```

Listing 7-5. Waiting for Input Field to Be Enabled After Clicking Enable Button

```
it('TC123_waitForEnabled', () => {
    browser.url('https://the-internet.herokuapp.com/
    dynamic_controls')
    var elem = $('input[type="text"]')
    $('button=Enable').click()
    elem.waitForEnabled({
        timeout: 10000
    })
    console.log($('#message').getText())
})
```

197

Output

It's enabled!

```
$(selector).waitForEnabled({ timeout, reverse, timeoutMsg,
interval })
```

It also detects when the element is no longer enabled in DOM. Refer to Listing 7-6.

Listing 7-6. waitForEnabled() Method With Reverse Parameter Set to True

```
elem.waitForEnabled({
    reverse: true
})
```

Wait for an Element to Exist

This command waits till the element gets rendered in the DOM before letting the control go further. As you can see in Listing 7-7, we wait for element h4 to exist before printing it in the console. Once the Start button is pressed, as shown in Figure 7-4, the element is rendered in the DOM in few seconds. It is fetched via getText and displayed in the terminal through console.log.

Dynamically Loaded Page Elements

Example 2: Element rendered after the fact

Start

Figure 7-4. Start button displays Hello World!

Syntax

```
waitForExist()
```

Listing 7-7. Waiting For Input Field to Exist in Web Page DOM After Clicking Finish Button

```
it('TC124_waitForExist', () => {
    browser.url('https://the-internet.herokuapp.com/
    dynamic_loading/2')
    var elem = $('#finish')
    $('button=Start').click()
    elem.waitForExist({
        timeout: 7000
    })
    console.log('TEXT IS ' + $('#finish').$('<h4 />').
    getText())
})
```

199

Output

```
TEXT IS Hello World!
```

waitForExist has the following parameters.

```
$(selector).waitForExist({ timeout, reverse, timeoutMsg,
interval })
```

It also detects when the element is no longer enabled in DOM, when the page is reloaded, or any changes to the page due to an AJAX call. Refer to the example in Listing 7-8.

Listing 7-8. waitForExist() Method With Reverse Parameter Set to True Which Waits Until the Element Cease to Exist in DOM

```
elem.waitForExist({
    reverse: true
})
```

Wait Until

waitUntil is a go-to command for all wait operations in WebdriverIO. As shown in Listing 7-9, it expects a condition and waits until that condition is fulfilled with a *truthy* value before letting the control pass on. It's an explicit and fluent wait. It imposes a condition and a timeout and allows the user to set the polling operation interval and a message to display if the timeout happens. These parameters are forwarded to the waitUntil method by the options object.

Syntax

```
browser.waitUntil({ options, timeout, timeoutMsg, interval })
```

Listing 7-9. waitUntil Method with Timeout, Timeout Message, Polling Interval

```
it('TC125_Wait Until', () => {
    browser.url('https://the-internet.herokuapp.com/
    dynamic_loading/1')
    $('button=Start').click()
    var elem = $('#finish')
    browser.waitUntil(function () {
        return (elem.isDisplayed())
    }, {
        timeout: 15000,
        timeoutMsg: 'expected text to be different after 15s',
        interval: 200
    })
    console.log('TEXT IS ' + $('#finish').$('<h4 />').
    getText())
})
```

Output

```
TEXT IS Hello World!
```

An explicit wait in WebdriverIO takes in a condition and waits for it to be fulfilled (see Figure 7-5). The wait is a specified timeout period. During this time, polling occurs at certain intervals to check if the condition is fulfilled. If it's not fulfilled, a timeout message is thrown.

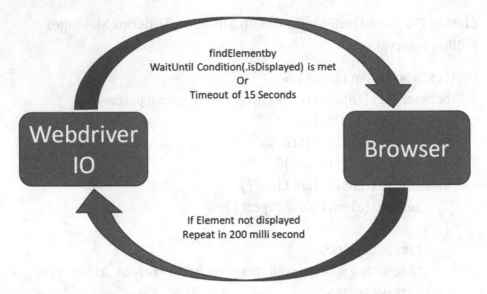

Figure 7-5. *Polling mechanism of waitUntil example in Listing 7-9*

Summary

This chapter looked at hard wait and an explicit waits. If you have a background in Selenium, you must have observed that implicit wait was missing. Implicit waits are applied over the entire time the browser session is open, so it's an overall wait rather than an element-specific wait.

The next chapter looks at an implicit wait implemented in the form of a timeout in WebdriverIO. It also looks at other timeouts in WebdriverIO.

CHAPTER 8

Timeouts

In the last chapter, you learned about waits, which play a very important part in making tests stable. On the other side of the spectrum, if a test case fails, it should fail as quickly as possible.

A specified time is allowed to elapse in a test script before an error message is displayed to the user; this is called the *timeout period*. If there is a failure during the test, timeouts ensure that it happens as quickly as possible, ending with a timeout message so the user doesn't have to wait indefinitely and blocking the rest of the test execution. Timeouts also ensure that the control moves on to the next command instead of waiting for an indefinite amount of time for the current command to complete.

This chapter studies different types of timeouts, their causes, and how you can avoid them. On a high level, it covers the following.

- How to get and set timeouts
- Selenium-related timeouts
  - Implicit wait timeout
  - Page load timeout
  - Session script timeout
- WebdriverIO-related timeouts
  - WaitForTimeout

© Shashank Shukla 2021
S. Shukla, *Practical WebDriverIO*, https://doi.org/10.1007/978-1-4842-6661-8_8

- Framework-related timeouts
  - Mocha
  - Jasmine
  - Cucumber

Setting and Getting Various Timeouts

browser.setTimeouts({ implicit, pageLoad, script }) is a command that can set three different timeouts at the same time. It is mentioned in the describe block, as shown in Listing 8-1.

Listing 8-1. Command to Set and Get Implicit, Pageload and Script Timeout

```
describe('Webdriver.io examples', () => {
    browser.setTimeouts(8000, 9000, 5000)

    it('TC126_Display GetTimeout', () => {
        browser.url('https://webdriver.io')
        console.log(browser.getTimeouts())
    })
})
```

Output

```
{ implicit: 8000, pageLoad: 9000, script: 5000 }
```

Through this command, you can set implicit, pageLoad, and script timeouts to 8, 9, and 5 seconds, respectively. Make sure you don't copy the code in Listing 8-1 because that results in your code having two describe blocks, one inside the other. Let's look at this next.

Session Implicit Wait Timeout

An implicit wait is implemented as a timeout in WebdriverIO; it is known as a *session implicit wait timeout*. It specifies the time to wait during a session when locating elements using the findElement or findElements commands ($ or $$, respectively). It is 0 milliseconds—unless stated otherwise.

In Listing 8-2, you state the implicit timeout as 5 seconds, or 5000 milliseconds. In Figure 8-1, the attempt to find the element lasts only 5 seconds (10:02:59 to 10:03:04) before an Element Not Found error is thrown. Keep your logLevel: 'info' in the wdio.conf.js file to observe this in the console.

Listing 8-2. Command to Set Implicit Timeout

```
it('TC127_SetimplicitTimeout', () => {
    browser.setTimeout({ 'implicit': 5000 })
    browser.url('https://the-internet.herokuapp.com/')
    $('<h3>').getText()
})
```

```
[0-0] 2021-01-01T10:02:59.927Z INFO webdriver: COMMAND findElement("tag name", "h3")
[0-0] 2021-01-01T10:02:59.927Z INFO webdriver: [POST] http://localhost:9515/session/2f523b8a42b
2021-01-01T10:02:59.927Z INFO webdriver: DATA { using: 'tag name', value: 'h3' }
[0-0] 2021-01-01T10:03:04.948Z INFO webdriver: RESULT {
  error: 'no such element',
  message: 'no such element: Unable to locate element: {"method":"tag name","selector":"h3"}\n'
```

Figure 8-1. Time start of element search to end

As with implicit waits in other frameworks, it is applied at the browser level once defined and works on all lines of code.

Implicit and explicit waits do not go well together, so you need to be cautious when using both in your code. Selenium.dev states: "Warning: Do not mix implicit and explicit waits. Doing so can cause unpredictable wait times. For example, setting an implicit wait of 10 seconds and an explicit wait of 15 seconds could cause a timeout to occur after 20 seconds."

Session Page Load Timeout

This is a Selenium timeout associated with the web page's time to completely load for the first time. Listing 8-3 sets it to 2 seconds. This means WebdriverIO allows only 2 seconds for the GitHub page to load, and if it doesn't load, it fails. This timeout is not realistic, but it does show the error received when a pageLoad timeout occurs (see Figure 8-2).

Listing 8-3. Command to Set Pageload Timeout

```
it('TC128_SetpageLoadTimeout', () => {
    browser.setTimeout({
        'pageLoad': 2000
    })
    browser.url('https://github.com/')
})
```

Output

```
2020-12-31T10:09:06.506Z INFO webdriver: DATA { url: 'https://github.com/' }
[1609409348.518][SEVERE]: Timed out receiving message from renderer: 1.081
[1609409348.519][SEVERE]: Timed out receiving message from renderer: 1.081
[0-0] 2020-12-31T10:09:08.516Z ERROR webdriver: Request failed with status 500 due to time
out: timeout: Timed out receiving message from renderer: 1.081
  (Session info: chrome=87.0.4280.88)
[0-0] timeout in "Webdriver.io examples TC128_SetpageLoadTimeout"
timeout: Timed out receiving message from renderer: 1.081
```

Figure 8-2. *Timeout error message of pageLoad timeout*

Unless stated otherwise, it defaults to 300,000 milliseconds.

Session Script Timeout

Under the hood, WebdriverIO is asynchronous. Asynchronous commands are non-blocking. A command does not wait for the previous command to be completed if it is waiting for a server response. Each session has an associated session script timeout that specifies the time to wait for the asynchronous scripts to run and finish. Listing 8-4 manually sets to 10 seconds but holds the script with an asynchronous blocking method for 15 seconds making the test case fail with error 'script timeout' as shown in Figure 8-3.

Listing 8-4. Command for Script Timeout

```
it('TC129_SetSessionScriptTimeout', () => {
    browser.setTimeout({
        'script': 10000
    })
    browser.url('https://www.google.com')
    browser.executeAsync((done) => {
        console.log('Blocking Asynchronous Function')
        setTimeout(done, 15000)
    })
})Output
```

```
2020-12-31T10:27:40.823Z INFO webdriver: DATA {
  script: 'return ((done) => {\n' +
  "            console.log('Blocking Asynchronous Function')\n" +
  '            setTimeout(done, 15000)\n' +
  '        }).apply(null, arguments)',
  args: []
}
[0-0] 2020-12-31T10:27:50.846Z ERROR webdriver: Request failed with status 500
due to script timeout: script timeout
  (Session info: chrome=87.0.4280.88)
[0-0] script timeout in "Webdriver.io examples TC129_SetSessionScriptTimeout"
script timeout
```

Figure 8-3. *Timeout error message of session script timeout*

Unless stated otherwise, a timeout is 30 seconds by default in Selenium.

WebdriverIO-related Timeouts: waitforTimeout

waitforTimeout is associated with the waitFor group of commands, such as waitForClickable and waitForDisplay. This timeout is configurable outside a test file. You can configure it as shown in Listing 8-5, where it is 15 seconds, or 15000 milliseconds, in the wdio.conf.js file. You can override it from the test file. Listing 8-6 overrides the timeout to 10 seconds, or 10000 milliseconds. (Note the lowercase f in waitforTimeout! See Figure 8-4.).

Listing 8-5. waitforTimeout Configuration in wdio.conf.js File

```
// wdio.conf.js
exports.config = {
    // Default timeout for all waitFor* commands.
    waitforTimeout: 15000,
    //
}
```

Listing 8-6. Overriding waitforTimeout from Test File

```
it('TC130_waitforTimeout', () => {
    browser.url('https://the-internet.herokuapp.com/')
    $('<h3>').waitForExist({ timeout: 10000 })
})
```

Output

```
[0-0] 2020-12-31T11:15:37.591Z INFO webdriver: COMMAND findElements("tag name", "h3")
[0-0] 2020-12-31T11:15:37.594Z INFO webdriver: [POST] http://localhost:9515/session/85
8741d620a9ea562c06f1f0948eb5e9/elements
2020-12-31T11:15:37.594Z INFO webdriver: DATA { using: 'tag name', value: 'h3' }
[0-0] Error: In "webdriver.io examples TC129_SetSessionScriptTimeout"
Error: element ("<h3>") still not existing after 10000ms
```

Figure 8-4. *Timeout error message of waitforTimeout*

Framework-related Timeouts

The Mocha framework organizes and runs test cases serially, but there are other frameworks compatible with WebdriverIO. To set framework-related timeouts, you can use the conf.wdio.js file's framework option, as shown in Listings 8-7, 8-8, and 8-9 for Mocha, Jasmine, and Cucumber, respectively. When a script takes longer to execute than what is specified in Mocha's timeout option, the script fails. The error is shown in Figure 8-5.

Listing 8-7. Mocha Timeout

```
// wdio.conf.js
exports.config = {
    // ...
    framework: 'mocha',
```

```
mochaOpts: {
    timeout: 20000
},
// ...
}
```

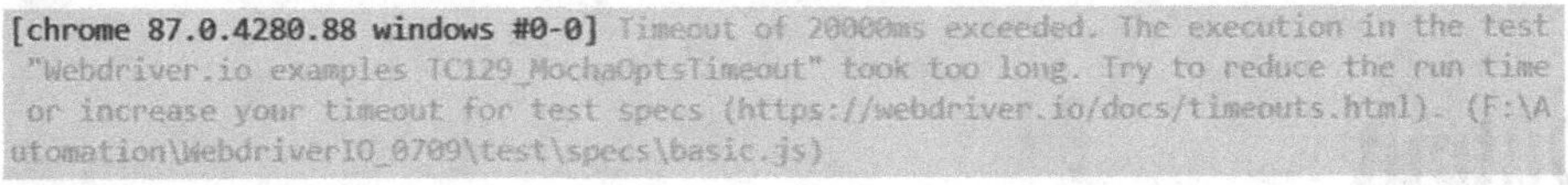

[chrome 87.0.4280.88 windows #0-0] Timeout of 20000ms exceeded. The execution in the test "Webdriver.io examples TC129_MochaOptsTimeout" took too long. Try to reduce the run time or increase your timeout for test specs (https://webdriver.io/docs/timeouts.html). (F:\A utomation\WebdriverIO_0709\test\specs\basic.js)

Figure 8-5. *mochaOpts timeout error message of*

Listing 8-8. Jasmine Timeout

```
// wdio.conf.js
exports.config = {
    // ...
    framework: 'jasmine',
    jasmineNodeOpts: {
        defaultTimeoutInterval: 20000
    },
    // ...
}
```

Listing 8-9. Cucumber Timeout

```
// wdio.conf.js
exports.config = {
    // ...
    framework: 'cucumber',
    cucumberOpts: {
        timeout: 20000
    },
    // ...
}
```

The testing framework that you use with WebdriverIO deals with timeouts, especially since everything is asynchronous. It ensures that the test process doesn't get stuck if something goes wrong.

By default, the timeout is 20 seconds, which means that a single test or it block should not take longer than that.

Summary

In this chapter, you saw Selenium, WebdriverIO, and framework-related timeouts. Next, let's explore framework options for integrating with WebdriverIO.

CHAPTER 9

Framework Options and Design Patterns

The last chapter looked at timeouts, including framework-related timeouts. WebdriverIO can be used with different types of frameworks. Choosing a framework depends on many different factors. In this chapter, you look at the frameworks compatible with WebdriverIO. This chapter covers the following.

- Frameworks introduction

- WebdriverIO with Cucumber

- WebdriverIO with TypeScript

- WebdriverIO with Jasmine

- WebdriverIO with Mocha

- Page Object Model design pattern introduction

Introduction to Frameworks

A framework is an organized code structure that maintains the code to make a test project simpler and more efficient. This is done by breaking code into smaller pieces or modules, which are logical and complete from their own perspectives.

© Shashank Shukla 2021
S. Shukla, *Practical WebDriverIO*, https://doi.org/10.1007/978-1-4842-6661-8_9

Take a house as a metaphor for a framework. You don't build a house with only one room. You segregate it according to the functionalities of the rooms. A kitchen is used for cooking and a bedroom is for sleeping—not the other way around. When you want to paint your kitchen, your bedroom is not impacted during the process. Similarly, a framework lets you know what changes need to be made.

WebdriverIO with Cucumber

Cucumber is a behavior-driven development framework (BDD). BDD is an agile development process that encourages close collaboration between developers, testers, and business analysts during a product development life cycle. This framework is used when testing high-level application behaviors. Business and product teams closely monitor and contribute to writing tests instead of developing unit tests.

Figure 9-1 shows the basic BDD process. Cucumber is also compatible with other programming languages.

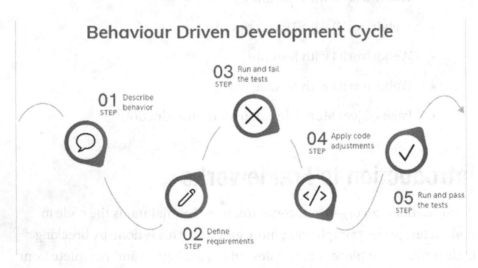

Figure 9-1. BDD development cycle (www.mobileappdaily.com/ behavior-driven-development)

The Cucumber framework is a boon, especially when your team closely collaborates with business analysts and product owners. The BDD assertion style that Cucumber provides using Gherkin is very business-friendly.

Given steps describe the initial context of the system—the *scene* of the scenario. It is typically something that happened in the *past*.

When steps describe an event or an *action*. This can be a person interacting with the system or an event triggered by another system.

Then steps describe an *expected* outcome or result.

If you have successive Givens, Whens, or Thens, you *could* also use And.

For further information, please go to the official Cucumber web site at https://cucumber.io/docs/gherkin/reference/.

Listing 9-1 shows a Cucumber test case written in the Gherkin language, which is available in the feature file. It is followed by its code in Listing 9-2, present in the steps file. Cucumber uses regular or its own expressions to link a Gherkin step in a feature file to its corresponding code in a step definition file.

Listing 9-1. Test Case in Features File in Cucumber Framework

```
Feature: Test the page title
    As a developer
    I want to be able to test if a page has a certain title

    Background:
        Given I open the site "/"

    Scenario: Test if the demo app has the title "DEMO APP"
        Given the title is "DEMO APP"
```

Then I expect that element "h1" contains the same text as element ".subtitle".

Listing 9-2. Corresponding Code in Step Definition File (Steps) in
Cucumber Framework

```
import { Given } from 'cucumber';

import openWebsite from '../support/action/openWebsite';

Given(
    /^I open the (url|site) "([^"]*)?"$/,
    openWebsite
);
import compareText from '../support/check/compareText';

const { Then } = require('cucumber');

Then(
    /^I expect that element "([^"]*)?"( not)* contains the same
    text as element "([^"]*)?"$/,
    compareText
);
```

The final folder structure of the BDD framework looks like Figure 9-2.

Figure 9-2. *How they are connected in the Cucumber framework*

For further reference, download the WebdriverIO boilerplate to integrate with Cucumber at `https://github.com/webdriverio/cucumber-boilerplate`.

WebdriverIO with TypeScript

Although JavaScript is a great programming language, it is fundamentally a functional programming language and not an object-oriented one, at least before the ES6 updates were available. Hence, many programmers prefer TypeScript as their go-to language with WebdriverIO. TypeScript is not a framework. It is compatible with Mocha, Jasmine, and Cucumber. TypeScript has the syntax of an object-oriented language because it is object-oriented JavaScript customization that can be compiled with JavaScript. TypeScript codes are easily maintainable, and developers are less likely to make syntactical mistakes because it is strongly typed language.

WebdriverIO with Jasmine

Jasmine is like an elder brother to Mocha. It was created around 2008. As the official documentation taglines say, it is "fast and has "batteries included." It provides testers with all the out-of-the-box features to test their software. The basic philosophy of this framework the use of behavior-driven development. In Listing 9-3, Jasmine's and Mocha's syntax are the same. The first parameter provides a plain English description of the test case. The Jasmine framework has its own assertion library.

Listing 9-3. Jasmine Way of Organizing the Tests

```
describe("A suite is just a function", function() {
  var a;
  it("and so is a spec", function() {
    a = true;
    expect(a).toBe(true);
  });
});
```

WebdriverIO with Mocha

Mocha is the framework used in this book. Mocha is a highly customizable framework. It doesn't aim to be a complete framework. Mocha provides developers a foundation and allows them to add custom extensions for assertions, code coverage, spies, fake data, reporting, and screenshots. This is why we integrate Chai, a popular assertion library, into the next chapter's framework.

Design Pattern Introduction

When designing a test framework, you must keep the test logic separated from the data and web elements. A design pattern is a reusable solution for commonly occurring problems. So far in this book, you have worked on one file (i.e., example.e2e.js or any other name that you chose to give it). Let's reuse an example from earlier chapters, as shown in Figure 9-3.

Figure 9-3. *OrangeHRM login page*

Listing 9-4 has its respective code. If you observe the code, you can label the pieces into different categories. It has a URL that is like an app-wide function, and part of it remains the same, regardless of which part of the web site is automated. It has locators like #txtUsername, which is from the web page. It has test data as well, like Admin and admin123. It has functions that help the user achieve actions (e.g., setValue, Click). It also has a generic or base pause function. Finally, it has an assertion necessary to verify the validation point. You also feel that the code is clunky and hard to read.

Listing 9-4. Respective it Blocks of the Login Page of Orange HRM
Web Site

```
it('To validate the alternate text of the logo is
"OrangeHRM"', () => {
    browser.url('https://opensource-demo.orangehrmlive.com/')
    $('#txtUsername').setValue('Admin')
    $('#txtPassword').setValue('admin123')
    $('#btnLogin').click()
    browser.pause(3000)
    var logo = $('img[src*="logo"]')
    expect(logo).toHaveAttribute('alt', 'OrangeHRM')
})
```

Let's try to fix it using the Page Object Model (POM), a design pattern
commonly used in Selenium for automating test cases. This design pattern
can be used with keyword-driven, data-driven, and hybrid frameworks.
POM directs each web page in the application to have a corresponding
page class. The elements of a web page are variables inside that class, and
the actions to be performed on the elements are methods of the class. The
naming conventions require that the elements be easy to read and related
to the tasks they perform.

The first step in optimizing our code is to make base.js and testdata.js
in the framework. Also, since we are automating a landing page and a login
page, let's create their respective pages (e.g., landing.page.js and login.
page.js).

This means your framework looks like Figure 9-4.

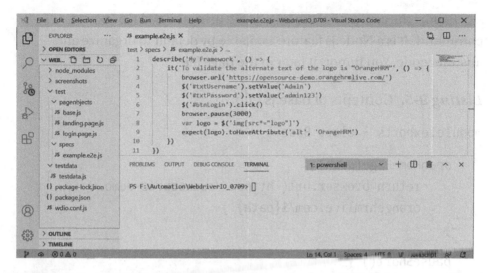

Figure 9 1. *Framework snapshot after creating all the necessary files and folders*

You are also using ES6 features provided by JavaScript, like the Class keyword. ES6 is also known as ECMAScript 6 or ECMAScript 2015, and it is a newer version of JavaScript with enhanced features.

Now let's try to understand the relevance of each file.

base.js

The base.js file contains all the helper methods, which are web page-agnostic. This means the methods are used across the web application. This file is inherited by all the page files, which can access the generic methods of the web app. The web app's URL is always constant. It is a good idea to separate the example.e2e.js file from the base.js file.

Create a class named Base inside base.js. A JavaScript class is syntactic sugar and doesn't correlate to what a Java class. A JavaScript class is a function behind the curtains. You define a method inside the class named openHomePage(), where you mention the web page's base URL. Listing 9-5 has all the contents of the base.js file.

Export the contents of the base.js file using the `module.export` command. It is a Node.js feature available by default to organize and abstract code. You import it later in the page file.

Listing 9-5. Contents of base.js File

```
module.exports = class Base {

    openHomePage(path) {
        return browser.url(`https://opensource-demo.
        orangehrmlive.com/${path}`)
    }

    pauseShort() {
        return browser.pause(3000)
    }

}
```

login.page.js

The login.page.js file has a LoginPage class that extends the Base class from base.js file via the required keyword, meaning it inherits the base page's methods. The LoginPage class has locators, methods, and overridden parent class methods. Locators are defined using the getter function. Getter has wider use but, in this context, a getter provides simpler syntax by avoiding () while accessing the method.

Methods are all the actions being performed on the page (e.g., setValue and click). You override the parent methods to adapt to the page class. The login.page.js file is shown in Listing 9-6.

Listing 9-6. Contents of login.page.js File

```
const Base = require('./base');

class LoginPage extends Base {
    get LoginInputBox() {
        return $('#txtUsername')
    }

    get PasswordInputBox() {
        return $('#txtPassword')
    }

    get LoginButton() {
        return $('btnLogin')
    }

    fillUsername() {
        return this.LoginInputBox.setValue("Admin")
    }

    fillPassword() {
        return this.PasswordInputBox.setValue("admin123")
    }

    clickLoginButton() {
        return this.LoginButton.click()
    }

    openHomePage() {
        return super.openHomePage('')
    }
}

module.exports = new LoginPage()
```

landing.page.js

Some parts of the end-to-end test case in Listing 9-4 spill over to the web app's landing page after the login step, where you verify the logo's alternate text attribute on the landing page (see Figure 9-5).

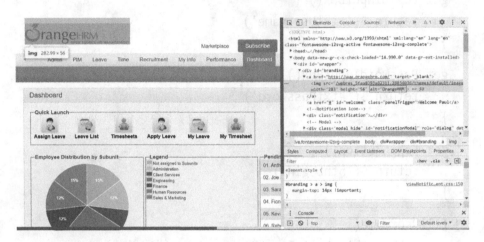

Figure 9-5. *Landing page logo attribute verification*

You need to capture the elements in this new page (i.e., landing page), in a new page object file named landing.page.js. This file also requires the base.js file. It has a class named LandingPage. This class has the logo's element locator strategy and a function that makes the assertion. The function is not hard-coded. The parameters are provided by the user from the examples.e2e.js file to maintain flexibility. Lastly, this file is exported, so it can be "required" in example.e2e.js. The contents of the landing.page. js file is shown in Listing 9-7.

Listing 9-7. Contents of landing.page.js File

```
const Base = require('./base');

class LandingPage extends Base {

    get logo() {
        return $('img[src*="logo"]')
    }

    verifyAttributes(alt, text) {
        expect(this.logo).toHaveAttribute(alt, text)
    }

}

module.exports = new LandingPage();
```

example.e2e.js

An example.e2e.js file requires the .page.js files and transform Listing 9-4 to Listing 9-8. The differences are notable.

Listing 9-8. Contents of login.page.js File

```
const LoginPage = require('../pageobjects/login.page')
const LandingPage = require('../pageobjects/landing.page')

describe('My Login application', () => {
    it('To validate the alternate text of the logo is
    "OrangeHRM"', () => {
        LoginPage.openHomePage();
        LoginPage.fillUsername()
        LoginPage.fillPassword()
        LoginPage.clickLoginButton()
```

```
        LoginPage.pauseShort()
        LandingPage.verifyAttributes('alt', 'OrangeHRM')

    })
})
```

EXERCISE

There is room for improvement and optimization in our framework. Integrate the following functionalities into their respective files in the framework.

1. Add a browser.debug() helper function.

2. Add a screenshot helper function.

3. Add a 10-second pause named longPause().

4. Test data admin and admin123 should be abstracted to their own separate files.

5. Add a new function for asserting the logo element's height and width.

6. Add a "forgot password" journey (the base URL needs to be appended with the "forgot password" link).

Summary

https://webdriver.io/docs/boilerplate.html provides some nice boilerplate WebdriverIO frameworks that the community's active members have created and contributed to. I encourage you to look at other frameworks on WebdriverIO web site. Figure 9-6 provides a high-level comparison of these frameworks.

Features	WebdriverIO With			
	Mocha	Jasmine	Typescript	Cucumber
Programming language	JavaScript	JavaScript	Typescript	JavaScript
Category	Unit Testing, Intergration Testing, End-to-End	Unit Testing, Intergration Testing, End-to-End Testing	Unit Testing, Intergration Testing, End-to-End Testing	Acceptance Testing
General info	Simple, flexible, fun javascript test framework for node.js & the browser	DOM-less simple JavaScript testing framework. Jasmine is a "batteries included" Behavior Driven Development testing framework for JavaScript	TypeScript extends JavaScript programming language by adding types. Types provide a way to describe the shape of an object, providing better documentation, and allowing TypeScript to validate that your code is working correctly.	Cucumber is a software tool that supports behavior-driven development.
Licence	Open Source	Open Source	Open Source	Open Source with Pro option
Framework Type	Hybrid	Hybrid	Hybrid	Hybrid
Assertions	Not available	Built in	Not available	Built in
Promise Support	Available	Available	Available	Available

Figure 9-6. *Comparison of WebdriverIO when integrated with different frameworks*

WebdriverIO is compatible with a lot of frameworks. Since you use the Mocha framework in this book, we must use an external assertion library because Mocha doesn't have its own. Most automation testers use Chai as their go-to option for assertion because of its options. Let's look at assertion commands in the next chapter so that you can use assertions in a test case to validate the outcome against expectations.

CHAPTER 10

Assertions

In automation, validations in test scripts are also called *assertions*. Some WebdriverIO assertions were covered in Chapter 4 (i.e., element APIs). Node.js has a built-in assertion library that is called with `const assert = require('assert')`. No installation is required. However, you can implement more powerful assertions with the user-friendly Chai Assertion Library in your framework. Install Chai using `npm install chai -save--dev` at a terminal.

Once installed, import the Chai Assertion Library using statement `const assert = require('chai').assert` statement in the topmost line of your test file, as shown in Figure 10-1.

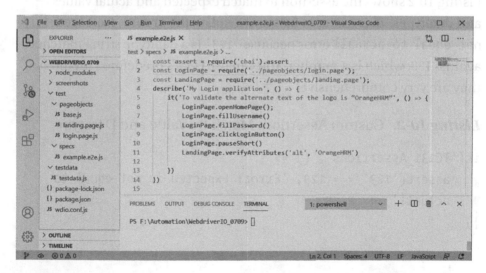

Figure 10-1. *Requiring Chai library in example.e2e.js file*

You can create custom assertions in Chai. Let's look at some examples.

© Shashank Shukla 2021
S. Shukla, *Practical WebDriverIO*, https://doi.org/10.1007/978-1-4842-6661-8_10

Determining If Strings Match by Value

Listing 10-1 shows that you can create a custom assertion and error message using the assert command. This assertion matches expected and actual values. It passes because the expected and actual values are the same (i.e., 123).

Listing 10-1. Custom Assertion, Match By Value

```
it('TC130_Assertions', () => {
    assert('123' == 123, 'ERROR::- Expected != actual!')
})
```

Determining If Strings Match by Value and Type

Listing 10-2 shows the assertion to match expected and actual values and datatypes. This example fails and displays the Error: Expected is not equal to actual! error because '123' is a datatype string matched against 123, which is a number. You can use Chai's predefined methods; they are very comprehensive.

Listing 10-2. Custom Assertion, Match By Value and Datatype

```
it('TC131_Assertions', () => {
    assert('123' === 123, 'Error: Expected is not equal to
    actual!')
})
```

Determining If a Value Is Truthy

The word *truthy* means something "tends" to be true, if not completely true. In Listing 10-3, the expected value on the left-hand side is "a random string" that passes the assertion as truthy. 100, True, and { } are examples of truthy values.

Listing 10-3. Asserting Actual to Be Truthy

```
it('TC131_Assertions', () => {
    assert.isOk("a random string", "Error: Expecting Truthy
    value-")
})
```

Determining If a Value Is Falsy

Listing 10-4 shows a falsy value. It passes if you provide values like null, "", 0, undefined, and NaN because they are also falsy values.

Listing 10-4. Asserting Actual to Be Falsy

```
it('TC133_Assertions', () => {
    assert.isNotOk(false, "Error: Expecting Falsy value-")
})
```

Determining If a Value Is Equal (==)

Listing 10-5 checks if the value on the right-hand side matches the value on the left. The script fails and displays the Error: expected 'Available Examples' to equal 'Available Example' error because 'Available Example', was expected but the actual header is 'Available Examples' (see Figure 10-2).

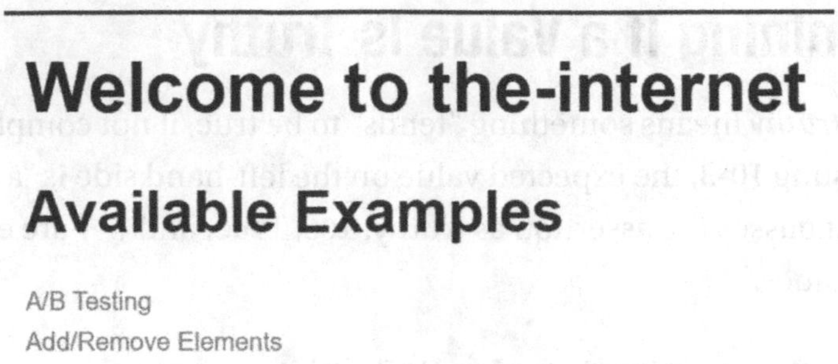

Welcome to the-internet

Available Examples

A/B Testing
Add/Remove Elements

Figure 10-2. *Heroku home page header*

Listing 10-5. Asserting a Value to Be Equal

```
it('TC134_Assertions', () => {
    browser.url('https://the-internet.herokuapp.com/')
    var elem = $('<h2>').getText()
    assert.equal(elem, 'Available Example', "Error")
})
```

Determining If a Value and Type Both Are Equal (===)

Listing 10-6 fetches the h2 tag name attribute. However, the name attribute is not available for h2, so you get a null value, which is a datatype in JavaScript. If you try to assert it to 'null', which is a string, it fails and displays the Error: expected null to equal 'null' error because strictEqual expects the datatype to match along with the values.

Listing 10-6. Asserting Value and Type to Be Equal

```
it('TC135_Assertions', () => {
    browser.url('https://the-internet.herokuapp.com/')
```

```
    var elem = $('<h2>').getAttribute('name')
    assert.strictEqual(elem, 'null', "Error")
})
```

Determining If a Value Is Not Equal (==)

Listing 10-7 is set to fail with Error: expected 'Available Examples' to not equal 'Available Examples' because the expected and actual values are the same.

Listing 10-7. Asserting Value Not to Be Equal

```
it('TC136_Assertions', () => {
    browser.url('https://the-internet.herokuapp.com/')
    var elem = $('<h2>').getText()
    assert.notEqual(elem, 'Available Examples', "Error")
})
```

Determining If a Value and Type Are Not Equal (==)

Listing 10-8 passes because the expected and actual values are equal. Their datatypes are not equal because one is a string, and one is a number. The test case passes although they are not strictly equal.

Listing 10-8. Asserting Value and Type Both Not to Be Equal

```
it('TC137_Assertions', () => {
    assert.notStrictEqual(3,"3",'Error: Expected should not ===
    Actual')
})
```

Determining If a Value Is Higher Than Expected

Listing 10-9 determines if the number of links on the Herokuapp home page is greater than 100. The example most likely fails because 46 links (or <a> tags) were found when I executed the command.

Listing 10-9. Asserting Value to Be Greater Than

```
it('TC138_Assertions', () => {
    browser.url('https://the-internet.herokuapp.com/')
    var elem = $$('<a>').length
    assert.isAbove(elem, 100, 'Error: actual should be greater
    than expected.')
})
```

Determining If a Value Is Lower

Listing 10-10 is similar to Listing 10-9 but determines if the number of links on the Herokuapp home page is less than 100. It passes the execution because there are less than 100 links.

Listing 10-10. Asserting Value to Be Smaller Than

```
it('TC139_Assertions', () => {
    browser.url('https://the-internet.herokuapp.com/')
    var elem = $$('<a>').length
    assert.isBelow(elem, 100, 'Error: actual should be greater
    than actual.')
})
```

Determining If Expected Is True

Listing 10-11 shows the workings of the isTrue assertion. The script passes if Boolean 'true' is present. Be advised, 'true' does not work since it's a string, not a Boolean. Here it fails, showing the Error: Expecting True: expected 'true' to be true error.

Listing 10-11. Asserting Value Is True (Boolean)

```
it('TC140_Assertions', () => {
    assert.isTrue(true, 'Error: Expecting True')
})
```

Determining If Expected Is False

Listing 10-12 shows the workings of the isFalse assertion. The script passes if a Boolean false is present. Be advised, 'false' does not work because it's a string, not a Boolean. The script fails with the Error: Expecting False: expected 'false' to be false error.

Listing 10-12. Asserting Value Is False (Boolean)

```
it('TC141_Assertions', () => {
    assert.isFalse(false, 'Error: Expecting False')
})
```

Determining If Expected Result Is an Array

The assertion in Listing 10-13 determines if the expected result is an array.

Listing 10-13. Asserting Value Is an Array

```
it('TC142_Assertions', () => {
    var menu = ['green', 'chai', 'Mocha'];
    assert.isArray(menu, 'Error: Expected Array Element')
})
```

Determining If an Actual Result Is a String

The assertion in Listing 10-14 determines if the actual result is a string. Since h2 in the internet.heroku web page is a string, the test case passes.

Listing 10-14. Asserting Value Is a String

```
it('TC1143_Assertions', () => {
    browser.url('https://the-internet.herokuapp.com/')
    var elem = $('<h2>').getText()
    assert.isString(elem, 'Error: Expected a String')
})
```

Determining If an Array Contains a Value

The assertion in Listing 10-15 determines if the array contains the specific value that the user is expecting.

Listing 10-15. Asserting Array Contains Specific Value

```
it('TC144_Assertions', () => {
    assert.include([1, 2, 3], 2, 'Error: Element not found')
})
```

Verifying the Length of an Array

The assertion in Listing 10-16 verifies the length of an array. The code fails with the `Error: Array length unexpected: expected [ Array(46) ]` `to have a length of 50 but got 46` error.

Listing 10-16. Asserting Length of an Array

```
it('TC145_Assertions', () => {
    browser.url('https://the-internet.herokuapp.com/')
    assert.lengthOf($$('<a>'), 50, 'Error: Array length
    unexpected')
})
```

Summary

This chapter looked at Chai assertion commands. There are other assertion libraries, like Jasmine's built-in assertion, power-assert, and expect.js.

In the next chapter, you learn how to parallelly run test cases and reporting.

Verifying the Length of an Array

The assertion in Listing 10-16 verifies the length of an array. Had code fails with the Error: Array length does not, expected [Array(10)] to have a length of 10 but got 4 or so.

Listing 10-16. Asserting Length of an Array

```
it('TC163. Assertions', () => {
  browser.url('https://the-internet.herokuapp.com/')
  assert.lengthOf($$('a'), 50, 'Expected Array length
  unexpected')
})
```

Summary

This chapter looked at WDI assertion commands. There are other assertion libraries available. These are built-in assertion, browser.assert and
assert.

In the next chapter you'll run build run integrated, run test cases and
pipelines.

CHAPTER 11

Configuration File

So far in our automation journey, you have interacted with the wdio.conf.
js file in a limited capacity. Now that you can smoothly design and execute
test cases in WebdriverIO, and you understand the basics of framework
designing, it's time to familiarize yourself with some of WebdriverIO's
configuration settings. All configurations are listed in the wdio.conf.js file.
Let's go through some of these settings and discuss major functions, such
as reporting and parallel execution in WebdriverIO.

This chapter covers the following.

- Runner setting
- Path to test files via the specs parameter
- How to exclude files via the exclude parameter
- logLevel parameter
- Reporting
  - reporters
- Parallel execution
  - capabilities parameter
  - maxInstances parameter

© Shashank Shukla 2021

S. Shukla, *Practical WebDriverIO*, https://doi.org/10.1007/978-1-4842-6661-8_11

Runner

WebdriverIO can run on multiple platforms. The runner setting lets the you communicate where you want to run test cases in WebdriverIO. Figure 11-1 shows the setting in the wdio.config.js file.

```
1    exports.config = {
2        //
3        // =====================
4        // Runner Configuration
5        // =====================
6        //
7        // WebdriverIO allows it to run your tests in arbitrary locations (e.g. locally or
8        // on a remote machine).
9        runner: 'local',
10       //
```

Figure 11-1. *Runner configuration setting*

Figure 11-2 shows the options provided during installation for running tests. I used a local machine in this book; however, you can also integrate WebdriverIO with cloud services like Sauce Labs and BrowserStack.

You can find more references at the following web sites.

- https://webdriver.io/docs/browserstack-service.html

- https://webdriver.io/docs/sauce-service.html

- https://experitest.com/mobile-app-testing/
  how-to-get-started-using-with-webdriverio-with-
  experitest/

```
PS F:\Automation\WebdriverIO_0709> cd .\node_modules\
PS F:\Automation\WebdriverIO_0709\node_modules> cd .\.bin\
PS F:\Automation\WebdriverIO_0709\node_modules\.bin> wdio config

==========================
WDIO Configuration Helper
==========================

? Where is your automation backend located? (Use arrow keys)
> On my local machine
  In the cloud using Experitest
  In the cloud using Sauce Labs
  In the cloud using Browserstack or Testingbot or LambdaTest or a different service
  I have my own Selenium cloud
```

Figure 11-2. WDIO test runner config wizard

Specs

The specs parameter or setting tells WebdriverIO where your test files are located. The value shown in Figure 11-3 tells WebdriverIO to look for all files that have a .js extension in all the folders available under specs folder, which is located inside the test folder in the root directory.

```
11     // ==================
12     // Specify Test Files
13     // ==================
14     // Define which test specs should run. The pattern is relative to the directory
15     // from which `wdio` was called. Notice that, if you are calling `wdio` from an
16     // NPM script (see https://docs.npmjs.com/cli/run-script) then the current working
17     // directory is where your package.json resides, so `wdio` will be called from there.
18     //
19 v   specs: [
20         './test/specs/**/*.js'
21     ],
```

Figure 11-3. WDIO config file specs parameter

Exclude

The exclude parameter bars the test runner from picking up files that are mentioned in the value. Figure 11-4 mentions the spec_2.js file in the exclude parameter. In the console log, only spec_1.js is executed.

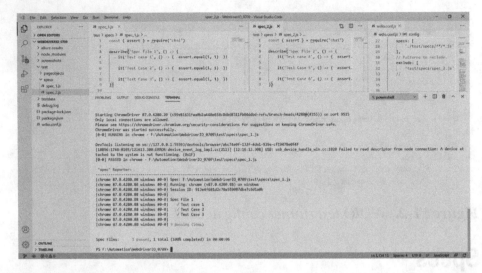

Figure 11-4. *WDIO config file exclude parameter*

logLevel

You can control the amount of information seen in the console terminal with the logLevel parameter. As shown in Figure 11-5, it produces information on each step executed by the runner.

```
69      // Level of logging verbosity: trace | debug | info | warn | error | silent
70      logLevel: 'info',
71 ∨    //
```

Figure 11-5. *WDIO config file logLevel parameter*

Services

WebdriverIO provides service integration to run your tests. Figure 11-6 shows the ChromeDriver service.

```
107      // Test runner services
108      // Services take over a specific job you don't want to take care of. They enhance
109      // your test setup with almost no effort. Unlike plugins, they don't add new
110      // commands. Instead, they hook themselves up into the test process.
111      services: ['chromedriver'],
```

Figure 11-6. *WDIO config file services parameter*

Many other services can be integrated with WebdriverIO, as shown
in Figure 11-7. There are differences among these services. selenium-
standalone needs a middleman (known as a *browser driver*) to handle
requests and responses back and forth from the browser to WebdriverIO/
Selenium automation scripts. These browser drivers are unique with
respect to browser support and are released by the browser makers.

- ChromeDriver (Chrome)

- geckodriver (Firefox)

- IEDriver (Internet Explorer)

- Edge WebDriver (Edge)

- Chromium Edge WebDriver (Edge Chromium)

If you are automating only the Chrome browser, you can use the
ChromeDriver service provided by the WDIO test runner. However,
according to Chrome DevTools protocol, WebdriverIO/Selenium can
directly communicate with the browser running in debug mode, making
automation straightforward. This is not recommended for cross-browser
testing because DevTools are developed by the Chrome development
team, and might throw unexpected results when handling other browsers.
TestingBot, Applitools, Sauce, and BrowserStack are cloud service
providers that can host testing and make cross-browser testing easier.

```
? Do you want to add a service to your test setup? (Press <space> to select,
<a> to toggle all, <i> to invert selection)
>(*) chromedriver
 ( ) sauce
 ( ) testingbot
 ( ) selenium-standalone
 ( ) devtools
 ( ) applitools
 ( ) browserstack
(Move up and down to reveal more choices)
```

Figure 11-7. *WDIO config wizard services*

Reporters

WebdriverIO provides integration with different reporter services. By default, the spec reporter is installed with the initial setup. You can verify it in the wdio.conf.js file by looking at the reporter's parameter, as shown in Figure 11-8.

```
130        // Test reporter for stdout.
131        // The only one supported by default is 'dot'
132        // see also: https://webdriver.io/docs/dot-reporter.html
133        reporters: ['spec'],
```

Figure 11-8. *WDIO config file 'reporters' parameter*

Multiple reporters can be integrated at the same time. Some of the available reporter options are shown in Figure 11-9.

```
? Which reporter do you want to use? (Press <space> to select, <a> to toggle all, <i> to invert selection)
>(*) spec
 ( ) dot
 ( ) junit
 ( ) allure
 ( ) sumologic
 ( ) concise
 ( ) reportportal
(Move up and down to reveal more choices)
```

Figure 11-9. *WDIO config wizard for reporter*

Allure is a popular reporting tool that produces beautiful reports after test execution. Let's install this tool and generate a sample report.

```
npm i @wdio/allure-reporter@6.10.6 --save-dev
```

Add the code in Listing 11-1 to the wdio.conf.js file (see Figure 11-10).

Listing 11-1. Example.e2e.js File Contents for Reporter Demo

```
exports.config = {
    // ...
    reporters: [['allure', {
        outputDir: 'allure-results',
        disableWebdriverStepsReporting: true,
        disableWebdriverScreenshotsReporting: true,
    }]],
    // ...
}
```

Create a folder named allure-results in the root directory of your project.

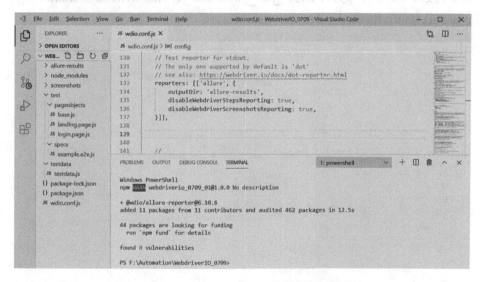

Figure 11-10. *Framework after integration with Allure*

245

Run your example.e2e.js file content using wdio.conf.js, as shown in Listing 11-2.

Listing 11-2. Example.e2e.js File Contents for Reporter Demo

```
const { assert } = require("chai")

describe('Demo of Allure Reporter', () => {
    it('Test case 1', () => { assert.equal(1, 2) })

    it('Test Case 2', () => { assert.equal(1, 1) })

    it('Test Case 3', () => { assert.equal(1, 1) })
})
```

Once the execution is completed, run 'allure generate allure-results -clean' followed by the 'allure open' command as shown in Figure 11-11. If you get an error that states, 'Please set the JAVA_HOME variable in your environment to match the location of your Java installation,' you must follow the steps at https://docs.oracle.com/cd/E19182-01/821-0917/inst_jdk_javahome_t/index.html to install Java and set up its environment variable.

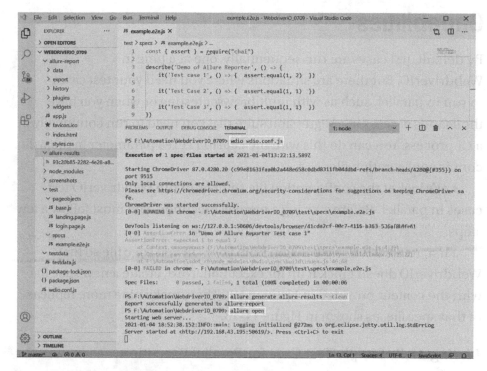

Figure 11-11. *Framework after integration with Allure*

In your browser, you see a test report for the three test cases, as shown in Figure 11-12.

Figure 11-12. *Allure report interface in browser*

Capabilities

By default, test cases are run sequentially, one at a time in WebdriverIO. But there are situations where you need your test cases to run in parallel, such as with multibrowser testing or when you have thousands of cases in a regression suite that you need to run continually in a CI process. You can do this with the `capabilities` parameter in the wdio. conf.js configuration file.

Let's look at the configuration file settings to run WebdriverIO test cases in parallel. Before starting a parallel execution, you must follow a few steps.

First, remove the .js extension from your current spec file so that WebdriverIO doesn't pick it up for execution. Next, create a new spec file with the content provided in Listing 11-3. Then, make nine more replicas of that spec file, as shown in Figure 11-13.

Listing 11-3. Simple Test Case for Parallel Execution

```
describe('Webdriver.io examples', () => {
    it('Parallel Execution', () => {
        browser.url('https://the-internet.herokuapp.com/')
        browser.pause(1000)
        console.log("Spec File executed")
    })

})
```

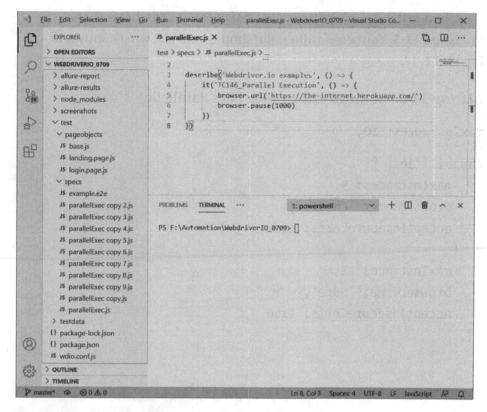

Figure 11-13. *Your framework should look like this*

Now that you have ten spec files, go to the wdio.conf.js file and find the maxInstances and capabilities parameters. They are set similar to Listing 11-4 in their default states.

Listing 11-4. Default wdio.conf.js Capabilities Settings

```
maxInstances: 5,
capabilities: [{
    maxInstances: 1,
    browserName: 'chrome',
    acceptInsecureCerts: true
}],
```

249

Change these settings from their default states to what is shown in Listing 11-5. Your conf.wdio.js file should look like what's shown in Figure 11-14.

Listing 11-5. Settings to Run Spec Files Parallelly

```
maxInstances: 10,

capabilities: [{
    maxInstances: 5,
    browserName: 'chrome',
    acceptInsecureCerts: true
}, {
    maxInstances: 5,
    browserName: 'edge',
    acceptInsecureCerts: true
}],
```

```
JS wdio.conf.js ×

JS wdio.conf.js > [∅] config
 28        // Capabilities
 29        // =============
 30        // Define your capabilities here. WebdriverIO can run multiple capabilities at the same
 31        // time. Depending on the number of capabilities, WebdriverIO launches several test
 32        // sessions. Within your capabilities you can overwrite the spec and exclude options in
 33        // order to group specific specs to a specific capability.
 34        //
 35        // First, you can define how many instances should be started at the same time. Let's
 36        // say you have 3 different capabilities (Chrome, Firefox, and Safari) and you have
 37        // set maxInstances to 1; wdio will spawn 3 processes. Therefore, if you have 10 spec
 38        // files and you set maxInstances to 10, all spec files will get tested at the same time
 39        // and 30 processes will get spawned. The property handles how many capabilities
 40        // from the same test should run tests.
 41        //
 42        maxInstances: 10,
 43        //
 44        // If you have trouble getting all important capabilities together, check out the
 45        // Sauce Labs platform configurator - a great tool to configure your capabilities:
 46        // https://docs.saucelabs.com/reference/platforms-configurator
 47        //
 48
 49
 50        capabilities: [{
 51            maxInstances: 5,
 52            browserName: 'chrome',
 53        }],
 54
 55        //
 56        // ====================
 57        // Test Configurations
 58        // ====================
 59        // Define all options that are relevant for the WebdriverIO instance here
 60        //
 61        // Level of logging verbosity: trace | debug | info | warn | error | silent
 62        logLevel: 'info',
```

Figure 11-14. *Your wdio.conf.js file should look like this*

Let's go over these options before you start parallel execution. The first maxInstances parameter (before the capabilities parameter) is the total number of browsers that WebdriverIO can spawn during execution. The maxInstances parameter inside the capabilities is the maximum Chrome browser instances that can be spawned. In this scenario, you only have a bandwidth of five more browser instances to spawn if you also add the Firefox browser to your capabilities.

Consider this, if you have one spec file and two capabilities (i.e., Chrome and Firefox) with the maxInstances parameter set to 1, the same spec file runs in Chrome and Firefox in parallel.

Let's suppose you have two spec files and two different capabilities (Chrome and Firefox). You set the maxInstances parameter as 2 for the WDIO spawn and 4 for the browsers (2 for Chrome and 2 for Firefox) to execute both files at the same time.

Figure 11-15 shows 10 spec files with one test case each and 10 total maxInstances—5 each for Chrome and Edge. Hence, you see 10 browsers spawning at any given time to run a few specs in Chrome and the next few in Edge.

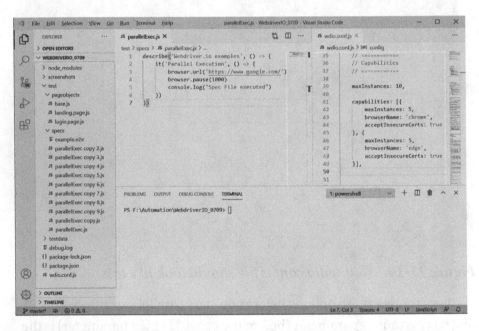

Figure 11-15. *Ten spec files distributed among two browsers running parallelly*

In the console log, you observe that the spec files were distributed among the two browsers, and at any given time, no more than five instances of each browser were open (see Figure 11-16).

```
Starting ChromeDriver 87.0.4280.20 (c99e81631faa0b2a448e658c0dbd8311fb04ddbd-refs/branch-heads/4280@{#355}) on p
ort 9515
Only local connections are allowed.
Please see https://chromedriver.chromium.org/security-considerations for suggestions on keeping ChromeDriver saf
e.
ChromeDriver was started successfully.
[1-3] RUNNING in edge - F:\Automation\WebdriverIO_0709\test\specs\parallelExec copy 5.js
[0-1] RUNNING in chrome - F:\Automation\WebdriverIO_0709\test\specs\parallelExec copy 3.js
[0-3] RUNNING in chrome - F:\Automation\WebdriverIO_0709\test\specs\parallelExec copy 5.js
[0-2] RUNNING in chrome - F:\Automation\WebdriverIO_0709\test\specs\parallelExec copy 4.js
[0-0] RUNNING in chrome - F:\Automation\WebdriverIO_0709\test\specs\parallelExec copy 2.js
[1-1] RUNNING in edge - F:\Automation\WebdriverIO_0709\test\specs\parallelExec copy 3.js
[0-4] RUNNING in chrome - F:\Automation\WebdriverIO_0709\test\specs\parallelExec copy 6.js
[1-4] RUNNING in edge - F:\Automation\WebdriverIO_0709\test\specs\parallelExec copy 6.js
[1-0] RUNNING in edge - F:\Automation\WebdriverIO_0709\test\specs\parallelExec copy 2.js
[1-2] RUNNING in edge - F:\Automation\WebdriverIO_0709\test\specs\parallelExec copy 4.js

DevTools listening on ws://127.0.0.1:54198/devtools/browser/d7e595d6-3638-4cdc-99b8-73ca46d425d5

DevTools listening on ws://127.0.0.1:54199/devtools/browser/549ad626-f816-4c91-9c56-a8e7bfa61680
```

Figure 11-16. *Console message logging the spawning and spec allocation activity of two browsers*

Summary

This chapter looked at a WebdriverIO file's configuration settings. You learned how to use them to make automation test cases more flexible and feature-rich. You saw how reporter and parallel testing works and discovered the configuration file's relevance.

The next chapter sums up your WebdriverIO automation journey by looking at some of the tool's pros and cons.

CHAPTER 12

Conclusion

You started your journey by setting up the WebdriverIO test tool, where you learned how to install the framework and its related dependencies and run a demo spec file. This was followed by methods to locate elements using the various selector strategies provided by WebdriverIO, which are essential to interacting with web elements.

Then you learned WebdriverIO APIs through very simple examples that enabled you to automate various user actions on located elements. You also learned useful assertion methods provided by WebdriverIO out of the box. You learned the importance of waits in automation testing and implemented various wait commands.

Next, you learned about timeouts, which are important in ensuring test case robustness. After covering enough groundwork, we touched upon various WebdriverIO framework options. You learned about the Page Object Model design pattern. Since WebdriverIO's assertions are not sufficient for testing real-world web apps, you learned some widely used Chai assertion commands. In the last chapter, you learned about WebdriverIO's configuration settings and how to integrate a reporter and execute tests parallelly by making changes to the configuration file.

I know there is still a lot to discover in using the WebdriverIO tool, but now you are well equipped to explore on your own.

Let's look at some of the advantages, disadvantages, and challenges associated with the tool as we wrap up.

© Shashank Shukla 2021
S. Shukla, *Practical WebDriverIO*, https://doi.org/10.1007/978-1-4842-6661-8_12

Advantages of WebdriverIO

- WebdriverIO runs on Selenium WebDriver, which means that it inherits Selenium's features. WebdriverIO is a JavaScript/Node.js implementation of the Selenium WebDriver API. It offers the power and flexibility of Selenium in your tests. You can verify this in the Dependencies section at npmjs.com, as shown in Figure 12-1.

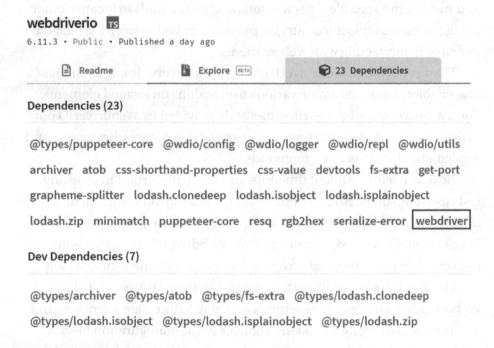

Figure 12-1. *WebdriverIO dependencies (www.npmjs.com/package/ webdriverio)*

- Parallel execution is easy to set up with a simplified wdio.conf.js file, as demonstrated in Chapter 11.

- WebdriverIO is highly flexible, letting you choose
  your favorite testing framework (Jasmine, Mocha, or
  Cucumber) and design pattern, as discussed in Chapter 9.
  External libraries like the Chai Assertion Library can be
  easily integrated, as you saw in Chapter 10, unlike other
  frameworks that try to enforce their assertion or reporting
  libraries. Figure 12-2 shows the reporters that integrate
  with WebdriverIO.

Reporter

Allure Reporter

Concise Reporter

Dot Reporter

Junit Reporter

Spec Reporter

Sumologic Reporter

Report Portal Reporter

Video Reporter

HTML Reporter

JSON Reporter

Mochawesome Reporter

Timeline Reporter

CucumberJS JSON Reporter

Markdown Reporter

Figure 12-2. *Reporter options that can be integrated into Wedbriverio*

- Synchronous implementation of asynchronous browser
  commands. You have not used complex JavaScript
  features like callbacks, async/await, or promises
  (mentioned in Chapter 1) to control the execution flow.

- Setting up and installing the framework is extremely simple for non-programmers with the help of the @wdio/cli command-line interface and customization with WDIO config wizard, as you saw in Chapter 1.

- It has a simpler syntax than Protractor (another JavaScript-based Selenium WebDriver API wrapper), selenium-webdriverjs (a vanilla WebDriverJS), and most other frameworks, as you saw in Chapters 3, 4, and 5.

- Selenium Server need not be started independently; it's managed by the framework. As you saw in Chapter 1, there were no additional steps to get a selenium server setup as it was managed by WebdriverIO internally.

- It has good support to identify shadow elements and react elements, as shown in Chapter 2.

- Waits and Timeouts are handled more effectively with easy-to-understand syntax, as you saw in Chapters 7 and 8.

- It easily integrates with many cloud services, as you saw in Chapter 11. Some of the services are shown in Figure 12-3.

Services

Appium Service	UI5 Service
Applitools Service	WireMock Service
Browserstack Service	Slack Service
Crossbrowsertesting Service	Intercept Service
Devtools Service	LambdaTest Service
Firefox Profile Service	Visual Regression Testing Service
Sauce Service	
Selenium Standalone Service	Ng-apimock Service
Shared Store Service	Novus Visual Regression Service
Static Server Service	Re-run Service
Testingbot Service	
Webdriver Mock Service	winappdriver Service
ChromeDriver Service	ywinappdriver Service
Zafira Listener Service	
Report Portal Service	
Docker Service	

Figure 12-3. `https://webdriver.io/docs/appium-service.html`

Disadvantages of WebdriverIO

- WebdriverIO API documentation can be overwhelming for beginners or people switching from Java-based test automation tools.

- It only supports JavaScript, which limits your options based on your programming language skills.

- The Robot class, Sikuli, AutoIT, and similar tools that automate Windows-based applications cannot be integrated into WebdriverIO. Windows application–based testing is not possible on WebdriverIO. Any tool based on Selenium WebDriver must run with WDIO to debug.

- It can be used for automating AngularJS apps, but it is not designed to work with Angular-based web apps as well as the Protractor tool, which is marketed as a go-to AngularJS automation tool.

- Since it is an open source tool, WebdriverIO has known issues open at any given time, which can be seen at `https://github.com/webdriverio/webdriverio/issues`.

Challenges of Using WebdriverIO

- It is sometimes hard to trace errors in WebdriverIO when a test fails, as you noticed scrolling through the console terminal trying to identify errors.

- The installation process covered in Chapter 1 can be a challenge if there are version compatibility issues among Chrome, Node.js, external libraries, and WebdriverIO. It is always recommended that you install the latest stable version of WebdriverIO and other external libraries, or install the versions that are known to be compatible with each other. Rare scenarios involving geolocations (covered in Chapter 3) can be challenging to automate and depend on your WebdriverIO or Chrome versions. There is no rich community support if you experience any issues.

This book doesn't intend to cover every aspect associated with the WebdriverIO automation tool. This book acts as a go-to API reference guide for WebdriverIO and an interview guide for people whose main interest is hands-on exploration that goes beyond basic knowledge.

Most WebdriverIO and automation testing proficiency comes from practice and experience. As you gain experience, you make better and more informed decisions on locator strategy selections, correctly apply waits, and use meaningful assertions among the ones discussed in this book.

I wish you good luck on your future WebdriverIO automation journey.

Index

A

alert() method, 97

APIs

    active element, 181, 182

    CSS property, 184, 185

    element HTML

        code, 189, 190

    element location, 186–188

    element property, 182–184

    element size, 188, 189

    page source, 181

    tag name, 186

Assertions, 229

    Chai library, 229

    data type

        equal (===), 232, 233

        not equal (==), 233

    strings, 230

    value

        array, 235–237

        equal (==), 231, 232

        equal (===), 232, 233

        falsy, 231

        higher, 234

        isFalse, 235

        isTrue, 235

        lower, 234

        not equal (==), 233

        truthy, 231

Assign Leave form, 172–174

B

Behavior-driven development
framework (BDD), 214

Browser APIs

    alerts, 97

        dismiss, 98, 99

        display cookies, 109

        reading message, 101

        sending message, 100

        set cookies, 112

    array of elements, 46–48

    browser fullscreen mode, 84

    click an element, 59, 60

    close browser, 96

    closing page, 94, 95

    datepicker field, 88, 89

    debugging, 42–44

    delete cookies, 110

    displaying cookies, 108, 110

    double click an element, 62

    drag/drop, 105, 106

© Shashank Shukla 2021

S. Shukla, *Practical WebDriverIO*, https://doi.org/10.1007/978-1-4842-6661-8

Browser APIs (*cont.*)

drop-downs, 102, 104

element into view, 58

frames, 92–94

fullscreen screenshot, 90

geolocation, 113–115

get element size, 79

getting and setting
Window size, 76–78

input field, 64

input field, clearing text, 69

interacting elements, 52, 53

last element, return array of
elements, 51

links, 54

map function, 55–57

mouse, 69, 70

navigates URL, 71

open new window, 85, 86

refresh web page, 74, 75

restart browser, 75, 76

right click an element, 63

$('selector').addValue
(value), 65, 66

set cookies, 111, 112

submitting form, 108

switching windows, 90, 91

text of element, 49–51

uploading file, 107, 108

URL/authentication, 44, 45

value of an element,
getting, 67, 68

Vanilla JS Code, 87, 88

browser.back() command, 72

browser.closeWindow()
command, 94

browser.debug()
command, 42, 88, 89

browser.deleteCookies()
command, 110

browser.forward() command, 73

browser.fullscreenWindow()
command, 84

browser.getActiveElement(), 181

browser.getAlertText()
command, 101

browser.getCookies()
command, 108

browser.getUrl()command, 86

browser.getWindowRect()
command, 76

browser.keys()
command, 66, 108

browser.maximizeWindow()
command, 80

browser.minimizeWindow()
command, 83

browser.refresh() command, 74

browser.reloadSession()
command, 75

browser.setCookies()
command, 111

browser.switchTo(Alert)
command, 98

browser.switchToWindow(handle)
command, 90

C

Capabilities
  Chrome/Firefox, 251, 252
  console log, 252, 253
  create spec file, 248
  framework, 248, 249
  maxInstances, 251
  removing.js extension, 248
  RunSpec files, 250
  spec files distribution, 252
  wdio.conf.js, 249, 251
Configuration file
  Exclude, 241
  Loglevel, 242
  Runner, 240, 241
  Services, 242, 244
  Specs, 241
Cucumber, 210, 214

D

Design patterns, 219
  base.js, 221, 222
  code, 219, 220
  example.e2e.js, 225
  framework, 220, 221
  landing.page.js, 224, 225
  login.page.js, 222, 223
  OrangeHRM login page, 219
  POM, 220
  user achieve actions, 219
Document Object
      Model (DOM), 20, 39

E

End-to-end test, 69, 70, 145, 146, 224

F

forEach() method, 52, 56
Framework-related timeouts
  Cucumber, 210
  Jasmine, 210
  Mocha, 209, 210
Frameworks, 213, 214

G

Geolocation, 113
getAttribute() method, 54, 183

H

Hard sleep, 192, 193

I

Intermittent ads, 144
isClickable()
  disable button, 141
  notes, 142
  output, 142
  syntax, 141
isDisplayed()
  notes, 131
  output, 130, 131
  start button, 129
  syntax, 130

isEnabled()
    disabled text box, 124, 125
    HTML code, 124, 126
    notes, 126
    output, 126
    syntax, 125
isExisting()
    console log, 120
    output, 119
    start button, 118
    syntax, 118
isFocused()
    input box, 148
    notes, 149
    output, 149
    syntax, 148
isSelected()
    checkboxes, 136, 137
    notes, 138
    output, 138
    syntax, 137

J, K, L

Jasmine, 210, 217, 218

M, N

map() method, 55
Mocha, 19, 209, 218

O

OrangeHRM logo, 171, 172

P

Page Object Model (POM), 9, 220

Q

querySelector() method, 39

R

React, 30, 36, 37
Reporters
    Allure, 245
    allure open command, 246
    example.e2e.js file
        contents, 245, 246
    framework, 245, 247
    options, 244
    parameter, 244
    test reports, 247
rowser.deleteSession()
command, 96

S

$('selector').addValue(value), 65
$('selector').clearValue()
        command, 68
$(selector).getCSSProperty
        (cssProperty)
        command, 184
$(selector).getHTML({ })
        method, 189
$(selector).getLocation(prop)
        method, 186

$(selector).getProperty(property)
command, 182

$('selector').getSize()
command, 79

$(selector).getSize(prop)
method, 188

$(selector).getTagName()
command, 186

$('selector').setValue("")
command, 64

Selenium-related timeouts
implicit wait timeout, 205
page load timeout, 206
script timeout, 207

Session implicit wait timeout, 205

Shadow DOM
errorText, 175
front-end design, 176
HTML code, 176, 177
JSFiddle, 175, 176
output, 178–180
purple, 175
syntax, 177
vs. regular, 176

switchToParentFrame command, 94

T, U, V

Timeouts
Cucumber, 210
Jasmine, 210
Mocha, 209, 210
session implicit wait
timeout, 205, 206

session page load
timeout, 206
session script timeout, 207, 208
setting/getting, 204
waitforTimeout, 208, 209

toBeChecked()
checkboxes, 140
output, 140
syntax, 139

toBeClickable()
notes, 143
output, 143
syntax, 142

toBeDiplayedInviewport()
notes, 135
output, 134
syntax, 134

toBeDisabled()
disabled input box, 128
notes, 129, 133
output, 129, 132
syntax, 128, 132

toBeElementsArrayOfSize()
notes, 170
output, 170
synatx, 170

toBeEnabled()
notes, 127
output, 127
syntax, 127

toBeExisting()
notes, 124
output, 124
syntax, 123

toBeFocused()
  expect() keyword, 149
  notes, 150
  output, 150
  syntax, 150
  websites, 150
toBePresent()
  notes, 123
  output, 122
  syntax, 122
toBeSelected()
  checkboxes, 138
  output, 139
  syntax, 138
toBeVisible()
  output, 134
  syntax, 133
toBeVisibleInViewport()
  elements, 135, 136
  output, 136
  syntax, 135
toExist(), 120
  notes, 121
  output, 121
  syntax, 120
toHaveAttribute()
  <a> tag, 151
  <img> tag, 152, 153
  nots, 152
  output, 152–154
  syntax, 151, 153
toHaveAttributeContaining()
  notes, 155
  output, 155

syntax, 154
toHaveClass
  <h1> header tag, 155, 156
  notes, 157
  output, 156, 157
  syntax, 156
toHaveClassContaining()
  jQuery menu, 157, 158
  notes, 159
  output, 158, 159
  syntax, 157
toHaveElementProperty()
  height property, 159
  notes, 160
  output, 160
  syntax, 160
  TagName locator, 159
toHaveHref()
  demo element, 162
  notes, 163
  output, 162
  syntax, 162
toHaveHrefContaining()
  output, 164
  syntax, 163
toHaveId()
  output, 169
  syntax, 168
toHaveLink()
  notes, 165
  output, 165
  syntax, 164
toHaveLinkContaining()
  notes, 166

output, 166
syntax, 165
toHaveText()
   notes, 167
   output, 167
   syntax, 166
   TagName selector, 167
toHaveTextContaining()
   output, 168
   syntax, 168
toHaveValue()
   demo element, 161
   notes, 162
   output, 161
   syntax, 161

W, X, Y, Z

Waits
   explicit, 191
   implicit, 191
   waitForClickable(), 193, 194
   waitForDisplayed(), 194–197
   waitForEnabled(), 197, 198
   waitForExist(), 198–200
   waitUntil, 200–202
WebdriverIO, 19
   advantages, 256–258
   APIs, 255
   challenges, 260
   chrome, 3
   Cucumber
      BDD framework, 216, 217
      BDD process, 214

feature file, 215
step definition file, 216
steps, 215
definition, 1, 2
disadvantages, 259, 260
installation process
   configuration, 9
   example.e2e.js file, 11
   json file, 7
   Node.js, 5
   node package manager, 7
   page object, 10
   terminal option, 6
   test, 12
   VS Code, 4
Jasmine, 218
Mocha, 218
Node.js/JavaScript-based
   framework, 13
TypeScript, 217
VS Code, 3
WebdriverIO command, 60
WebdriverIO-related
   timeouts, 208, 209
Web locators
   certain text, 30
   chain selectors, 35, 36
   class, 21, 22, 24, 25
   CSS query selector, 31
   custom selectors, 38, 39
   elements, 17
   framework, 17
   ID, 20
   JS function, 34

Web locators (*cont.*)
    link text, 28
    Mocha, 19
    name attribute, 25, 26
    partial link text, 29

    react selectors, 36, 37
    tag name, 26, 27
    Ultimate QA, 16
    XPath, 32, 33
Web pages, 16

Printed in the United States
by Baker & Taylor Publisher Services

Printed in the United States
by Baker & Taylor Publisher Services